TRANSFORMING AMERICA

Consulting Editor:

CHARLES H. PAGE
University of California, Santa Cruz

TRANSFORMING AMERICA

Patterns of Social Change

BY

RAYMOND W. MACK

Northwestern University

Random House : New York

FIRST PRINTING

© Copyright, 1967, by Random House, Inc.

All rights reserved under International and Pan-
American Copyright Conventions. Published in
New York by Random House, Inc., and simultane-
ously in Toronto, Canada, by Random House of
Canada Limited.

Library of Congress Catalog Card Number: 67-11696

Manufactured in the United States of America
by The Haddon Craftsmen, Inc., Scranton, Pa.

For Ann

Foreword

It has been said that our age is all motion and no direction. A century ago many thoughtful observers, newly armed with the evolutionary doctrines of Darwin in biology and with the stages of societal development posited by Comte, were sure that change in the Western societies with which they were concerned had a direction and that, on the whole, that direction was good. So Change became cumulative development in a continuous line, or Evolution, and Evolution represented movement to more complex, more perfect forms—thus, Progress. How optimistic, how naïve, it sounds to modern ears.

To say that we are now less certain of Progress is perhaps the understatement of the century. But if we have lost some of the confidence of the nineteenth-century exponents of Progress, we nevertheless retain the hope that increasing knowledge of human society and culture will help to focus intelligent efforts on diagnosing and dealing with many of the frustrating, painful, stultifying, unjust, or dangerous conditions of today and tomorrow. This hope finds increasing support in the advancement of research and certified knowledge in the social and behavioral sciences—uneven and tumultuous in development but exciting both in present yield and in promise for the future. Many of these specialized fields of study are advancing so rapidly that even the recently trained professional specialist has to struggle to stay abreast of just the main innovations.

In this situation, the only thing resembling a safe course for the social scientist is to specialize intensively, to speak cautiously, and to avoid currently controversial social issues.

Professer Mack will have no part of a sheltered sociology. In this book he prefers to lay his conclusions on the line in plain terms, unprotected by all the numerous technical and conceptual reservations and qualifications that would be at his disposal in the specialized publications designed for circulation primarily among other social scientists. He does not say, "Present evidence suggests that when normal adults are repeatedly exposed to abrupt changes in social norms, and to the rewards and punishments consequent upon conformity or nonconformity to these norms, in activities essential to realization of the most important life-goals of these individuals, there is a high probability of development of motor and/or affective disturbances in behavior patterns associated with such activities." Instead he says, "shifting standards of behavior make a man nervous." Although his blunt statement loses some scientific specificity, most readers will understand what he means and may well prefer his version.

Transforming America packs an impressive amount of information, analysis, and wisdom into a short book. To do so requires strict parsimony in exposition, restraint in appetite for details, and great skill in selecting the appropriate data.   Inevitably, not all the conclusions will be accepted by all readers, whether sociologists or not. In reading the original manuscript, I found myself impelled to enter a number of reservations and questions in the margins. (For example, I do not feel comfortable about descriptions of changes in income unless they are stated in terms of constant dollars.) But in the end, I had to admit that the queries and qualifications left the main messages intact and at the same time constituted an unpremeditated tribute to the empirical richness and challenging ideas to be found in these pages.

The author has not tried to write a "value-free" book —as if he does not care whether a particular social pattern or its opposite prevails. For example, it is clear that he respects individual uniqueness, rejects racial discrmination, and approves of personal freedom. One can agree or disagree, but there generally will be no difficulty in discovering where he stands. This is as it should be. His values do not get in the way of his objectivity or his critical regard for evidence, and, of course, that too is as it should be.

It is the duty and service of good sociology to show reality clearly—to make our society transparent to us. It is a privilege to help introduce a book that may contribute to that clarity of vision without which the people perish.

Ithaca, New York   ROBIN M. WILLIAMS, JR.
March, 1967

Preface

Is science responsible for much of the anxiety in modern life? What are the major social trends in the United States? What are the prospects for the American family? For the school and the student? For the labor force? What of the future role of government? Are Americans subject to too much pressure to conform? Some critics charge that Americans have lost their sense of purpose. What is the evidence?

The intelligent, educated citizen thinks about such questions and wants to be able to evaluate the evidence. But most people have neither the technical training nor the time to plow through the statistical research reports in professional journals in search of answers.

The purpose of this book is to summarize concisely what scholars have learned about social systems: families, groups, organizations, and nations. My aim is not to provide a set of facile answers, but to offer the thoughtful reader an opportunity to arrive at his own judgments based upon what facts social scientists have accumulated.

I have tried to assess carefully the data I have covered, usually following the consensus of the profession. For all but a few judgments, clearly labeled as personal and speculative, there is what I consider hard evidence.

I am grateful to my friend, Robert Dubin, who is my idea of a first-class sociologist. Professor Dubin read a draft of this book in manuscript, offered several helpful suggestions, and in general tried to keep me honest. My colleagues in the Department of Sociology at Northwestern University discussed the manuscript with me; I am especially indebted for their help and encouragement to Howard S. Becker, Arnold S. Feldman, Scott A. Greer, and Robert F. Winch. None of us ever knows the complete roster of those from whom he has taken ideas he thinks of as his own, but I am aware of my intellectual debts to several scholars: Kingsley Davis, George C. Homans, Everett C. Hughes, Floyd Hunter, Ralph Linton, Wilbert E. Moore, David Riesman, Richard L. Simpson, Richard C. Snyder, Melvin M. Tumin, and John Useem. For encouraging and believing in me, as well as teaching me, Harriet L. Herring and Rupert B. Vance have earned, I am confident, more gratitude than they know.

Perhaps a few words of explanation are in order about why I think we should do more of what I have tried to do here. Surely we social scientists have enough trouble sometimes communicating with one another so that one can argue that it is presumptuous in the extreme for us to try to discuss what we are up to with people who have not sat through seminars in Contemporary Sociological Theory and Advanced Methods of Social Research.

But I feel that we have an obligation to the society that supports our research and tolerates our odd interests, an obligation to share what we know and—more arguable but perhaps as important—an obligation to tell the public what we think is probably true given what we know.

Certainly work in social science should imbue one with a becoming modesty. We are probably better aware than some of our admirers of how much we don't know. But even a fair evaluation of our shortcomings can hardly be expected from a public that is uninformed or misinformed about our problems, assumptions, and interests. When I see the word "sociological" used as a synonym for "social" in newspapers and magazines, I suspect that some of the blame must devolve upon those of us who publish our findings in, say, the *American Sociological Review* but make no attempt to explain them to our friends in journalism. If lawyers, physicians, clergymen, political leaders, businessmen, or even university professors in the humanities make public statements about instincts, human nature, race differences, birth control, or the relationship between democracy and capitalism—and if we know these statements to be factually false—are we blameless? We are not, I think, to the extent that we treat our profession as a mystical priesthood of initiates. We are aware, of course, that the history of our own discipline helps to make us chary of taking public positions on social issues, but surely sociology is a mature enough undertaking by now that we need not hide behind a dogma of objectivity when confronted with questions of social fact and statistical probability.

All of us who have ever spoken to executives' clinics, P.T.A. meetings, church gatherings, or political discussion groups are aware that sociological sophistication has not been disseminated throughout even the better-educated strata of our society. We need only remind ourselves of the wealth of detailed misinformation about their world with which our freshmen arrive on campus each fall—even those with the advantage of well-educated parents. One reason is obvious: Most of what we know about the workings of society we have discovered since the parents of those freshmen completed their formal education. Look at the generalizations in an introductory sociology textbook, and note, in the footnotes to research findings, that most of those findings have been published within the past twenty years.

The purpose of this book is to summarize in nontechnical language the major social trends in the United States today. Social scientists know a great deal about what is happening in America to government, to industry, to schools, and to the family as a result of modern scientific work, but a large proportion of what they know is phrased in their technical code and buried in their professional journals. Both their private language and their private journals are highly useful to scholars in the social sciences, but neither helps them communicate to the rest of the citizens of the world—including their fellow scholars in the humanities and the physical sciences—what they are up to and what they have learned. This book, then, is not written for my fellow social scientists, but for other educated people who would like a broad overview of what social scientists know about current social trends.

Many of us in the fraternity are fond of complaining about the public recognition our work receives at the hands of popularizers. But, if we are dissatisfied with the journalists' mastery of our skills, we have no recourse but to make an honest attempt to learn theirs. Few among us are capable of doing the kind of job for our discipline that Clyde Kluckhohn did for anthropology with *Mirror for Man.* Perhaps we can never do as well as some of our friends, such as Stuart Chase. But, because we believe that sociology offers an important key to understanding the intricacies of human behavior, we should try.

RAYMOND W. MACK

Contents

TRANSFORMING
AMERICA

CHAPTER 1

The Scientific Revolution
and the Nervousness of Man

The plans and goals of the National Aeronautics and Space Administration had been presented to the citizens gathered in the auditorium. A question period followed. A lady in the audience challenged the speaker: "Instead of all you scientists trying to put a man on the moon, why don't you stay home and watch television as the good Lord intended?"

To this sweet lady and to millions like her, the intentions of the Almighty parallel closely her own preferences: the preservation of her present conveniences and the avoidance of disturbing change. It is not surprising, then, that she finds the past achievements of scientists and technicians splendid but views their current activities with apprehension and their future intentions with alarm.

If we view the knowledge accumulated by scientists as one large package, it seems silly to accept some of the contents and reject the rest, and we may laugh at the lady who wants to keep her television set but hopes not to see any rocket launchings on its screen. But, after a chuckle, we might pause to sympathize with her, for resistance to change is a normal human trait.

An invention, a new idea, any alteration in the established order makes it necessary for people to learn new ways of responding to new situations. The tendency of most of us most of the time is to avoid this stress and strain. Ladies who prefer television watching to lunar exploration have no monopoly on the feeling that life would be easier if science and technology would let well enough alone. The history of science is accompanied by a history of reactions to scientific discoveries—and a frequent reaction is opposition to innovation.

"Experts" are as capable of blind opposition to change as is anyone else. Doctors scoffed at the pioneer work of Louis Pasteur in bacteriology. United States naval officials were highly skeptical of John Ericsson's idea for a screw propeller. Commodore Cornelius Vanderbilt, the railroad magnate, dismissed George Westinghouse and his air-brake invention with the comment that he had no time to waste on fools. In 1906, the astronomer Simon Newcomb stated publicly that neither laws of physics nor the state of the industrial arts made it practicable for man to fly long distances through the air.

Sometimes resistance to change is clearly based upon the protection of vested interests. The owners of canal

4

barges and stagecoach lines vigorously opposed the construction of railroads. A century later, the railroad unions were attempting to thwart the introduction of the Diesel locomotive because it threatened the firemen's jobs.

But often simple fear of the unknown or reluctance to learn new patterns of behavior motivates a man to plump for the *status quo*. In the 1960s, literate citizens in metropolitan suburbs hold mass meetings to prevent competent local health officers from adding to the communities' water supplies the small amount of fluoride necessary to reduce tooth decay among the towns' children. The system of staggering the time for recess to allow more play space for the children had to be abandoned in one community because some parents who saw children on the playground all through the day spread the word that the new-fangled plan meant no work and all play.

Sociologists and psychologists have demonstrated time and again that ambiguity is a threat to security and emotional stability. People like to know what is expected of them. Uncertainty about the rules of the game makes people difficult to get along with; shifting standards of behavior make a man nervous. When, as in the southern United States, state law requires segregation of the races and Federal law forbids it, the resulting strain on individuals and organizations provides fertile ground for the seeds of conflict.

Indeed, when psychologists want, for experimental purposes, to turn a normal little white rat into a neurotic one, they simply change the rules of everyday life on him until he goes to pieces. They first teach the rat that, if he finds his way through a maze and trips a lever with his paw, he will receive a piece of cheese. Then the psychologists change the path of the maze. When the rat takes what used to be the correct turn to reach the lever and the cheese, he bumps into a wall. Suppose the little fellow has sufficient emotional strength to sustain this frustration and learn the new maze. Then he finally arrives at the lever, presses it with his paw, and instead of cheese receives an electric shock.

After enough such violations of what he has learned to expect as the normal operation of his world, a rat—even a hungry one—will lie at the beginning of the maze and stare. He will not even try to find the cheese.

Change is painful, but nevertheless human beings are possessed of a certain amount of curiosity. A little boy who is not searching for anything in particular will peer into a hole just to see what's there. This human characteristic, curiosity, sometimes has consequences that conflict with that other human tendency, resistance to change. The curiosity that led one of our ancestors to experiment with fire resulted in thousands of his fellows' altering their whole way of life: cooking and preserving their food, abandoning a wandering hunter's existence for life in settled communities, extending those settlements into colder climates, and eventually forging metal tools and weapons to replace crude stone implements. The questioning intellects of Copernicus and Galileo threw the solar system into a new perspective and forced men, in spite of their preference for traditional wisdom, to review their concepts, not only of physics and astronomy, but also of politics and religion. Few examples of the mental anguish inflicted upon men by science are more dramatic than the response of seventeenth-century thinkers to Copernicus' argument that the earth is not the center of the universe.

Even today, many people resist the implications of Darwin's now century-old observations about natural selection and the process of evolution. It is painful to abandon a view of man as slightly lower than the angels in favor of one that places him slightly higher than the apes.

Darwin, Copernicus, and the fire-tamer are bold examples, but each little increment of knowledge unearthed by scientists and applied by engineers is apt to cause dislocations in the carefully ordered existence of men. Gutenberg's movable type destroys the near-monopoly on written communication of the clergy and privileged classes. Television causes a crisis in the movie industry. The internal-combustion engine produces unemployment among buggy-whip makers. Home-permanent kits cause savings account withdrawals by beauticians. Oral contraceptives raise theological questions. The introduction of voting machines undermines carefully built metropolitan political organizations. Where science and its applications flourish, men, like the white rat in the maze, find the rules governing survival in a constant state of flux.

Science produces change, and change is difficult to accept. Never in human history have men lived in a more difficult century than this one. The rapid urbanization of the world is made possible through scientifically produced technologies, from death control through modern methods of sanitation, to the mass production of food on "factory farms." The striking growth of cities in the nineteenth and twentieth centuries has been a new experience in human history. World-wide urban expansion is bringing about great changes in the major patterns of social organization and culture.

Although cities existed 5,000 or 6,000 years ago, the

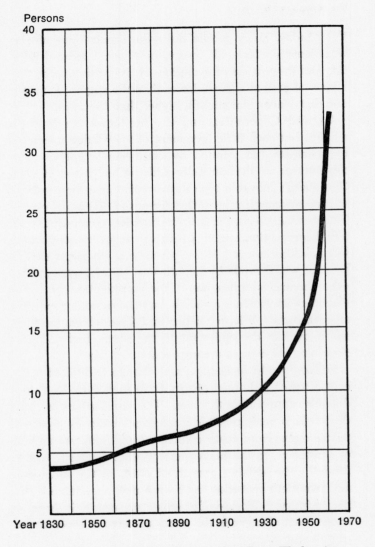

FIGURE 1. People Supplied by One Farm Worker in the United States, 1830–1970

SOURCE: U.S. Department of Agriculture, *Handbook of Agricultural Charts 1965* (Agricultural Handbook No. 300, 1966).

cities of the ancient world were generally small towns by modern standards. The largest of them contained only 1 or 2 per cent of the total population in their society, and Kingsley Davis estimates that it took from fifty to ninety farmers to produce the surplus needed to enable one man to live in an urban center. In fact, it is in the ratio of farmers to urban dwellers that the explanation can be found for the recency and suddenness of urbanization. Not until the Industrial Revolution—with its factory system, improved farming techniques, and tremendous speed-up in transportation of goods—was it possible for whole societies to become urbanized. Technological advances diminish the need for farm laborers. As can be seen in Figure 1, one farm worker's labor fed seven people in 1900. By 1950, one farm worker's labor fed nearly sixteen people. The latter figure more than doubled in fifteen years: By 1965 one farm laborer fed thirty-three people. Only when one farmer can raise enough food for many people can a society exist in which the majority of the people live in cities.

Only in the past century and a half has the world known truly urban *societies*, in which a high proportion of the total population lives in cities. As recently as 1800, only 2.4 per cent of the world's population lived in cities of 20,000 or more; today more than one-fifth of the people live in such cities. Furthermore, the proportion of people living in large cities has risen even more dramatically. By 1950 the proportion of people in the world living in cities was higher than that in even the most urbanized country in preindustrial times.

Between 1800 and 1850, the total population of the world increased only 29 per cent, but the population living in cities of 5,000 or more grew 175 per cent, that in cities of 20,000 or more by 132 per cent, and that in cities of 100,000 or more by 76 per cent. Then, from 1850 to 1900, the impact of scientific technology began to be felt in rapid industrialization. During that period, the total population of the world increased by 37 per cent. But, in the same span of time, cities of 5,000 or more increased by 192 per cent, those of 20,000 or more by 194 per cent, and those of 100,000 or more by 222 per cent. During the next half-century, from 1900 to 1950, cities expanded at an even more accelerated rate. While the population of the world increased by 49 per cent, the three size categories of urban populations grew 228, 240, and 254 per cent respectively.

If this trend continues at its present rate, more than a quarter of the world's people will be living in cities of 100,000 or more by the year 2000 and more than half by 2050. If the present rate of urbanization continues until the year 2050, more than 90 per cent of the world's people will live in cities of 20,000 or more.

Today we have whole societies that can be called "urbanized." More than four-fifths of the people in England live in urban places; nearly 40 per cent of them live in cities of more than 100,000. In societies like our own, with radio, television, rapid transportation, and an industrial distribution system, what is a fad on Manhattan Island today is a fad in Manhattan, Kansas, tomorrow.

The rate of change men have endured in the past 100 years is unparalleled in any previous time or place. The population of the world doubled between 1850 and 1930; at present rates of increase, it will double again between 1965 and 2000. The percentage of the world's population

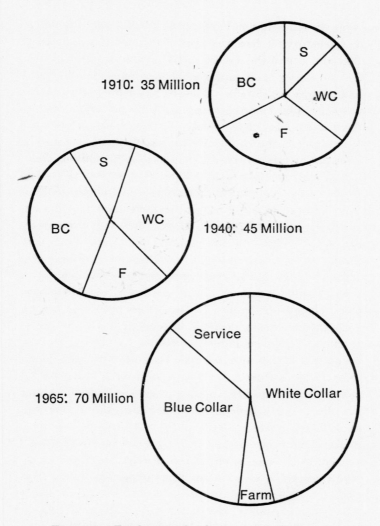

1910: 35 Million

1940: 45 Million

1965: 70 Million

FIGURE 2. Employment by Occupational Category in the United States, 1910–1965
SOURCE: U.S. Department of Health, Education and Welfare, Welfare Administration, Division of Research, *Social Development* (Publication No. 15, 1966), p. 10.

living in cities has more than doubled during the twentieth century; it has increased 500 per cent since 1850. Both the size of the American labor force and the proportion in clerical and professional jobs have doubled in a half-century, as shown in Figure 2, and the proportion of women in the labor force has nearly doubled. In 1900, there were only 238,000 students enrolled in colleges and universities in the United States. By 1950, there were 2.6 million. At present there are more than 5.4 million; there was an increase of nearly 80 per cent in the 1950–1960 decade alone. In Africa, there were four independent nations in 1950; twenty-two new states emerged in the ensuing decade. All these changes and many more—in population, migration, urbanization, the labor force, economic activity, education, and politics—are consequences, at least in part, of the discoveries and uses of science.

Small wonder that we have never before experienced so much change so rapidly: Never before in human history have so many men devoted so much effort to scientific research. Professor Purcell of Harvard estimates that 90 per cent of all the scientists who have ever lived are living today. We are investing more time, more energy, and more money in scientific activity than ever before. About $2 billion were spent on scientific research and development in the United States in 1945. The figure has risen steadily ever since; by 1961 it was $14.5 billion. Federal expenditures for research have multiplied 200 times in the past twenty-five years, from $74 million in 1940 to $15 billion in 1965.

In such a context, we can be certain of one thing: Change will continue to be rapid and far-reaching. As we have seen, swift and drastic change is unsettling. It constitutes a threat to individual security and to the stability of the social order.

For example, I recently interviewed a woman who is a department-store clerk in Chicago. She has customers she feels awkward in serving because they are wealthy, well-educated Negro women. She learned about Negroes from contact with cleaning women, as did most white Americans of her generation. She has had no instruction in or practice at dealing with Negro women who are the wives of insurance executives who make ten times as much money as she does.

Rapid social change, such as that in American race relations, poses various problems for different people. I also interviewed, about three years ago in Alabama, a poor, rural, uneducated southern Negro. He provides a model of what social scientists mean when they use the term "role conflict." This man grew up in a different world—a related one, but a different one—from that of the department-store clerk. He grew up in a world where there were two rules for survival: Don't make the white people mad; if in doubt, ask the minister.

Having learned that two basic rules are (1) don't irritate the white man, and (2) lean on the minister for advice, that Negro man goes to church Sunday morning and hears the minister tell him: "It is your duty as a good American citizen and as a Christian to do the following things, which are going to irritate white people: Go out there and protest; go and demand your rights; stand in line to register to vote." The *minister* is telling him to do these things. The poor man knows only two rules, and they are coming into direct conflict.

Social change is very hard on people because some of

the rules they have learned no longer count—but they can't always tell which ones they should abandon. Yet research also demonstrates that there is one way to mediate the threat, reduce anxiety, and overcome much human resistance to social change. Unlike the experimenters' white rats, human beings are able to learn to anticipate coping with situations they haven't lived through.

They are able, in other words, to understand change if it is explained to them. They can be told, "Something you have never experienced before is going to happen, and here's what it will be like." And they can mentally practice coping with it before it happens. Therefore they do not have to lie down at the beginning of the maze.

The key lies in understanding. The solution is to remove people from the category of the frustrated white rat by explaining what is happening and why it is occurring. Many studies in industrial sociology conclude that new policies and work patterns can be established with minimum personal insecurity and maximum ease of adjustment to change, if people are told what is happening and why.

Normal men and women everywhere deal with one another as members of groups. Only in the most exceptional cases do individuals survive in isolation, and such isolation is never absolute. Even a hermit has had some social experience. Every human being is born into a group and spends his lifetime in patterned social relations. Everything he does is closely bound up with what others do to and for him and with what others expect and accept from him. Each of us expects certain behavior from his relatives, friends, and even other human beings with whom he interacts only casually, say at a traffic intersection, and we are aware that others expect certain behavior from us in given situations. These facts indicate that group life is patterned.

It is, of course, possible to analyze what features make one group different from another: to contrast juries and friendship groups or to examine the range of variation among religious organizations. Indeed, some social scientists devote themselves to documenting the factors that make one society different from others. A large share of the research done by cultural anthropologists consists of descriptions of the unique: education among the African Tiv, agricultural practices of the Tikopia, social ranking among the Guatemalan Indians, religion in Madagascar, or trading patterns in the Andaman Islands.

Here, however, we shall devote our attention to the universal features of social life, concentrating on the things that all men do because they are human and social. To achieve this focus, we shall in the next chapter explore those activities in which it is essential for a society to engage simply in order to survive. When we have established a list of the necessities for social survival, we shall in subsequent chapters take the United States as a case study, and we shall chart social trends in each of these crucial areas of human activity. In this way, we can hope to gain perspective on the impact of science on a total social system in the areas where it matters most: the elements of social organization that must be present for the survival of the social system.

CHAPTER 2

Social Organization
and Survival

Any human society, if it is to survive, must be organized to accomplish five essential functions:

1. It must replace personnel when they die, leave, or become incapacitated;
2. it must teach new recruits to participate usefully, whether they are born into the society, migrate into it, or are hired or captured;
3. it must produce and distribute goods and services to keep its personnel going;
4. it must preserve order, so that its personnel are not keeping one another from the tasks of replacement, teaching, production, and distribution and so that they are not destroyed by hostile outside groups;

5. it must provide and maintain a sense of purpose among its members, so that they will be motivated to continue as members of the group and to satisfy the other four requirements for survival.

These five functions are necessary for the continuity, not only of a society, but also of any relatively permanent group. Smaller groups do not have to perform all these activities within their own boundaries. They must, however, be able to barter or otherwise arrange for the accomplishment of the same ends. A corporation, for example, does not have to supervise the biological reproduction of its executives and laborers (fortunately—it has enough problems as it is), but reproduction must take place in the larger society of which the corporation is a part so that there is a pool of potential personnel from which the corporation can recruit its executives and laborers. An adult friendship group does not have to teach its members to walk and talk, but somebody must, or there will not be desirable recruits for the group.

This list of universal functions appears to be a set of logical deductions, but it is more than that. Let us look at some of the evidence that each of these functions must be performed as the price of survival.

Replacing Personnel

Sexual reproduction is not, to be sure, the only method of bringing new members into a society. Annexation, the acquisition of slaves, and immigration are means of recruiting people. (Each of these three modes of population expansion has been used by the United States during its history.) Theoretically, it would be possible for a society to fill the positions of its dying members by recruiting replacements in one or more of these three ways from people born into other societies. The practical difficulty lies less in the recruitment than in the knowledge and loyalty required to maintain the social order. Teaching new members the basic cultural values and norms of a society is a task most readily accomplished when those new members are born into the society. Being entirely dependent for their survival on the adults in their primary group, small children are much more easily taught accepted behavior and attitudes than are adult immigrants or captives. In the days of frontier warfare, American Indians, who were aware of this fact, ordinarily took captive for induction into their society only young children, seldom adults.

For the bulk of its new members generation after generation, therefore, a society depends primarily on sexual reproduction.

There is no society that does not have a set of norms governing the reproduction of new members. Every culture contains some set of prohibitions, expectations, and rewards having to do with who should have children and the circumstances under which reproduction should occur.

The function of reproduction is so obvious that its crucial importance for societal survival is often overlooked. One is inclined simply to assume that all societies reproduce themselves. It is generally believed also that reproductive behavior is merely a natural biological phenomenon. Actually, the behavior patterns of human beings as they propagate their own kind are shaped and modified, as is their behavior in any other area of social life, by the culture through which they have been taught.

18

The basic act of procreation is influenced by the social norms concerning size of family, form of marriage, the sex act itself (whether it is considered exalted or shameful), marriage age, and economic obligations of parents toward their children.

The cultural values patterned around reproduction are enforced by both rewards and punishments. For example, we are critical of people whose families are notably larger than the norm, who "breed like animals," or who "just had another child and can't support the ones they have now." But we esteem people who have large families and hence have met their responsibility to society: "They gave two sons to the Church"; "The Beckers had four boys in service during the war." There is a definite feeling in American society that married couples are obligated to have children; people can be heard to speak disapprovingly of a couple with a big house and plenty of money who are "too selfish to have a family."

The emphases societies place on the reproductive function and the elaborate cultural regulations with which they surround it can be related to historical circumstances in which the power of any given group or tribe was directly related to the size of the society. When physical safety depended on the number of able-bodied warriors a tribe or nation could put into the field, every additional child was an important increment in the struggle for survival.

The Shakers (who, among other accomplishments, left their name on the Cleveland suburb of Shaker Heights) offer a striking example of the social cost of failure to replace personnel. The Shakers were a religious sect, one of whose tenets forbade sexual intercourse. So firmly were they committed to the sacredness of celibacy that male and female believers were segregated in separate dormitories. For a while the society prospered, recruiting converts to the faith. But as their proselytizing efforts became less effective and their commitment to sexual abstinence remained unshaken, their numbers dwindled. No replacement of personnel: no Shakers.

If a club cannot inspire joiners, if a corporation cannot recruit workers, if a society cannot replace its personnel, it cannot survive.

Teaching New Members

Procuring new members is not sufficient. These replacements must learn the ways of the group. They must be taught the basic values, or ethos, around which the normative system is organized. They must learn all the thousands of little behavior patterns that are accepted as normal in the society in which they are born: what to eat, how to eat it, where to eat it, when to eat it; what to wear, how to wear it, where to wear it, when to wear it; what to say, how to say it; and so on. Each new member must develop, sooner or later, a sense of self. He must learn to curb his own desires when they interfere with the reasonable expectations of others. He must, in short, adjust to social living.

Learning occurs both formally and informally. Going to school is part of the socialization process, and so is going to the movies. Overhearing a conversation in which someone is criticized teaches that one can avoid similar criticism by avoiding the behavior of the person under discussion. Education is a continuous process; when, at the age of eighty-two, a person learns something new about getting along in society, he is still being socialized. Education is cumulative: Learning to recognize the letters of the alphabet lays the groundwork for learning to comprehend written words, and reading written words enables one to learn still other things. Whenever we ask someone to give us new information in terms with which we are familiar—what a thing tastes like, what it feels like, what it is similar to—we are demonstrating the cumulative nature of learning.

Again, we have research evidence of the consequences of failing to teach new personnel how to participate in social life. Isabelle was an illegitimate child who was discovered in Ohio in November, 1938. Isabelle's grandparents, the parents of the unwed mother, were so ashamed of their daughter's having borne a child out of wedlock that they kept the mother and her little daughter secluded in a dark room away from the rest of the family and their friends and neighbors. Isabelle was virtually a cell in a controlled experiment, for her mother was a deaf-mute. For the first six years of her life, the child lived in almost total social isolation, lacking contact with normal human beings who could hear her or speak to her. When authorities learned of the situation, Isabelle was removed from this environment at six years of age and placed in the hands of child specialists. When she was found, Isabelle was rachitic, probably from improper diet and lack of sunshine. She could not speak but made certain croaking sounds. Her communication with her mother had been by simple gestures. Her reaction toward strangers, especially men, was almost that of a wild animal, revealing much fear and hostility. At first it was thought that she was deaf. Later, when it was found that she could hear, she was given various intelligence tests and pronounced feeble-minded. Her first score on the Stanford-Binet was nineteen months, practically a zero point on the scale. On the Vineland Social Maturity scale her initial score was thirty-nine—equivalent to that of a child of two and a half years.

Nevertheless, despite this poor performance, the specialists who had taken charge of Isabelle began a systematic program of training, beginning with pantomime and dramatization. Within a week Isabelle had progressed to her first try at verbalization. From a slow start, she picked up speed in her rate of learning and in a few weeks passed through the usual stages of learning for a normal child from ages one to six years. Within two years she had acquired knowledge and skills that ordinarily take six years to attain. By the time she was fourteen, Isabelle was in the sixth grade, socially and emotionally well adjusted, and doing well in her school work.

As Isabelle's case history illustrates, there is only one sensible answer to the old dormitory bull-session question: "Which is more important, heredity or environment?" The answer is "Yes." In the context of what social scientists know, the question is meaningless. An imbecile will remain an imbecile, regardless of the advantages of his environment. Environment cannot create traits that must be inherited through the genes. But heredity is a limiting factor, not a determining one. A potential genius can make no use of his mental capacities if he is reared in an environment as debilitating as Isabelle's was. A boy with an I.Q. comparable to Albert Einstein's who is born into an isolated tribe of illiterate Patagonians may invent a more efficient method of preserving food or discover a new use for fire, but he will not write a theory of relativity because his social environment does not equip him to tackle such a problem.

To participate in and contribute to the social order, a person must be taught to play a part in it. If a whole generation in a society were treated as Isabelle was, that society would perish.

Producing and Distributing Goods and Services

Many Americans speak of the United States as a "society founded on free enterprise" or as a "capitalistic nation." In a society that self-conscious about its economic life, it is hardly necessary to emphasize the fact that any ongoing social organization must make some provision for the production and distribution of goods and services. In a society without economic specialization each individual would work to satisfy his own wants, and no one would work to produce anything for anyone else. No such society exists. The fact that newborn members of a society are at first unable to provide for their own needs would in itself make such an arrangement impossible if the society were to survive.

Everywhere men have some set of norms ordering their activities so that the function of producing goods and services and distributing them will be performed. In even the most favorable environment, such social arrangements are necessary. Even where socially defined needs are minimal and natural resources are abundant, someone must be assigned the responsibility of picking the coconuts or berries for those unable to pick their own.

The price of failure in economic organization is clear in the history of famine. The weakened Eskimo family, exhausted and freezing without food, or the whitening bones of an unsuccessful Bushman hunter and his family in the South African desert are mute evidence of the necessity of production and distribution for survival.

Preserving Order

The natives of Tasmania were considered by their conquerors to be less than human, missing links half-way between apes and civilized men; British colonists organized hunting parties and shot Tasmanians out of the trees. The primitive weapons of the Tasmanians were no match for the tools of the English sportsmen; the Tasmanian aborigines have gone the way of the Shakers.

The social structure dear to the hearts of the nineteenth-century Russian nobility is as extinct as the social order of the Tasmanians. The Russian monarchy did not fall because of attackers from another society with superior weapons. It ceased to exist because it could not maintain order among the peasants, workers, sailors, and other less privileged members of the society.

Two facets of order are essential: A society must not destroy itself from within, and it must not allow itself to be destroyed by another society.

If a society were to reach the stage at which most of its members failed to abide by the basic rules, it would be doomed. If people were to kill one another wantonly, refuse to honor agreements, fail to fulfill social responsibilities, and mete out no punishment to those who ignored basic social norms, the society would soon cease to exist.

Anarchy may be a topic for philosophical discussions, but it is not a possible condition for social life.

Some deviance from the everyday rules occurs, of course, in every society. Every individual breaks some rule at one time or another, and some people self-consciously work at being rule-breakers: *les apaches* in Paris, Bohemians in Greenwich Village in one era and beatniks in another, the Sydney ducks of nineteenth-century San Francisco. Revolutionaries, too, are deviants from the norms of their time and place. Deviant behavior, then, can be an agent for introducing change, whether artistic fashion or political dogma. Deviance can help to preserve order, for it serves an escape-valve function. The Mardi Gras helps people to tolerate the deprivations of Lent. Inventors, scientists, artists, and political and economic innovators are all deviants to some extent. By showing new pathways and providing responses to pressures for change, they can help to maintain internal order in a society.

It is equally necessary that a society protect itself from outside attack. This point is hardly debatable: There are historical instances of societies that have perished through inability to maintain an order capable of resisting external pressures or attacks.

As ancient Carthage disappeared because of inability to withstand Roman might, so will any society or any group fail to survive if it cannot preserve internal and external order.

Providing and Maintaining a Sense of Purpose

Obviously, a society could not continue to exist if everyone decided that it was easier to quit than to go on. The

French sociologist Emile Durkheim made a fascinating study of one category of people who decide to quit, in which he concluded that what he called "anomic suicide" occurs most frequently in situations of *anomie*, a French word best translated as "without rules." A society without definite norms to regulate morals and social conduct is called "anomic." In an anomic situation, like a sudden economic depression, when the old rules no longer seem to apply and no new ones are immediately forthcoming, people do not know what is right and wrong or what the social expectations are, and they lose their sense of purpose. At such times, suicide rates are apt to soar.

The standard research techniques of the sociologist—observation, interviewing, and the questionnaire—are peculiarly unsuited to the study of people who have committed suicide. A considerable body of recent evidence suggests, however, that a lack of sense of purpose can cause the death of a man in ways more subtle than by his own hand. Both men and animals can have their motivation to continue so damaged that the physical mechanism itself simply quits.

Wild rats (sinking-ship clichés to the contrary) are capable of swimming for ninety hours or more. Nevertheless, if a rat is terrified in a laboratory and then plunged into water, he will die in a matter of minutes. Careful study of the rat's heart indicates that death is caused by a gradual depressive action of the nervous system. Contrary to the popular notion of being "scared to death," in the sense of a panic-induced speeding up of all the reflexes leading to excessive strain on the organism, what occurs is a gradual slowing of the heart's beat until the system quits operating. Furthermore, if the rat is removed from the water just before death, he recovers and is later able to swim as well as he did before being frightened.

Many physicians testify that they have seen inexplicable cases of death among patients who were profoundly depressed or filled with despair. Anthropologists, physiologists, and physicians who have studied cases of tribal "hexing" sometimes argue that, when people believe in "black magic," a hex may notably shorten life if not immediately kill a man.

The eminent neurologist Harold G. Wolff reports precise information from American war records demonstrating the impact of prolonged adversity on health and life span. Of approximately 6,000 United States prisoners of war captured by the North Koreans, about one-third died. According to medical observers, the cause of death in many cases was ill-defined; they call it "give-up-itis." Living in an environment of deprivation, a prisoner would become demoralized. Sunk in despair, he would become listless and apathetic. He would refuse to eat, to clean himself, or even to move. He would sit listless and staring and would finally die.

During World War II, about 94,000 American soldiers were taken prisoner in the European theater. They were imprisoned approximately ten months, on the average, and less than 1 per cent of them died in prisoner-of-war camps. In the Pacific, in contrast, the Japanese took about 25,000 American prisoners. They remained in captivity four times as long as those in Europe and suffered considerably more from humiliation, threats, and abuse. More than one-third of them died before liberation.

Six years after liberation, researchers re-examined those

who had survived Japanese prison camps. During the intervening six years, the total number of deaths in this group had been more than twice the expected incidence for a comparable group that had not suffered the prisoner-of-war experience. The causes of death included many diseases not directly related to imprisonment. Comparing deaths among the former prisoners with the death rate for a comparable sample of the population, nine times the expected number died of pulmonary tuberculosis. More than four times the expected number died from diseases of the gastrointestinal tract. More than twice the expected number died of cancer and twice the expected number of heart disease. Most impressive from the point of view of studying sense of purpose, twice the expected number committed suicide, and there were three times the expected number of deaths by accident. Among those who survived, the admission rate to veterans' hospitals was closely related to the amount of stress endured during imprisonment. Those who had "suffered greatly" had admission rates seven times as high as men who had not been prisoners.

As we try to comprehend the significance of maintaining a sense of purpose, it is especially useful to examine the cases of a few of the survivors who have, since liberation, become unusually effective citizens. These men, despite the deprivation they suffered, viewed imprisonment as a temporary interruption. They had long-range goals. They remained convinced that they would come out alive, and they continued to plan for the future. They were able to get some satisfaction out of life even while living under stress. They cultivated new interests. One prisoner, for example, raised rabbits for food and became interested in breeding them. The immediate distress seemed less real to these men because they focused their attention on life as they would live it in the future. They made elaborate plans for marriage, families, children, jobs, and they even plotted their recreation after liberation—where they would go and what they would eat. They formed cohesive groups, taught courses, had discussions, and even laughed together. Their maintenance of a sense of purpose kept the prison experience from sapping their vitality.

Although we know of no circumstances in which an entire society has perished through lack of motivation to continue, it is clear that an individual can be destroyed by extinguishing his will to carry on. As Wolff says, ". . . prolonged circumstances which are perceived as dangerous, as lonely, as hopeless, may drain a man of hope and of his health; but he is capable of enduring incredible burdens and taking cruel punishment, when he has self-esteem, hope, purpose, and belief in his fellows."

Crucial Questions for Americans

Let us now use each of these prerequisites for survival —replacement, education, production and distribution, order, and purpose—as a framework for examining the current state and prospects of the United States.

We shall consider, in the next five chapters, the American performance in replacing personnel, educating them, producing and distributing goods and services, maintaining social order, and sustaining a sense of purpose. By examining the trends in each of these areas, we shall try to see the impact of science on our way of life. As we sum up these trends and look at American society as a huge, complex social organization, what critical questions will come to the fore? What problems must we cope with if the United States as a social system is to survive?

To raise such a question is to place oneself in the tradition of Lester F. Ward, who, early in the century, offered a course at Brown University modestly entitled "A Survey of All Knowledge." But perhaps even a pretentious immodesty is more acceptable than a sterile conformity to the worst stereotype of the social scientist as a specialist who learns more and more about less and less until he is incapable of reaching a decision about anything. One department head in the Federal government has announced that, in the future, he will hire only one-armed social scientists—because he is so tired of having his staff answer his questions, "Well, on the one hand . . ."

What, then, can we conclude from our rapid tour of the United States as a social system? What are the questions that must be faced by responsible, educated American citizens? As we conclude each chapter on a function essential to social survival, we shall try to pose and analyze a crucial question confronting this generation of Americans.

CHAPTER 3

Births, Deaths,
and Families:
Traits and Trends

The replacement of personnel in any society, generation after generation, is a function of births, deaths, and migration. At present, most human societies run no risk of extinction from failure to replace their personnel. On the contrary, the population problem that contemporary societies face is that their numbers are increasing so fast that it is difficult to produce and distribute enough goods and services to maintain their present levels of living.

"The population explosion" has become such a common phrase that there is a danger that we may think we have explained it when we have only labeled it. When a man at a dinner party observes that he has read that the world's population will double within the next forty years, his partner murmurs, "Yes, the population explosion," and both nod thoughtfully as if *that* had been taken care of. The chances are that neither realizes that they are talking about one of the most obvious consequences of the scientific revolution. They may not think of the present rate of population growth as a result of applied science, but it is. What happened demographically when the work of scientists affected man's ability to stay alive?

Who Are All Those Others?

World population grew slowly until man learned to apply scientific knowledge in order to defer death. Two hundred years ago, after centuries of only slight increases, the population of the world began to expand at an unprecedented rate. In the nineteenth and twentieth centuries, the change has been even more impressive.

At the time of Christ, there were only about 250 million people on earth. By 1650 the estimated population of the world was between 465 and 545 million. Within the next 100 years it had risen to about 720 million. By 1850 it had reached 1.1 billion. It doubled again in eighty years, reaching 2 billion by 1930. World population is now more than 3.3 billion, triple that of a century ago.

This growth has not occurred uniformly over the earth. In 1950, when the world had 2.5 billion people, 800 million of them lived in the economically developed nations of North America, Japan, Europe, and the Soviet Union. Twice as many, 1.7 billion, lived in Africa, Asia, and Latin America. United Nations estimates, which are probably conservative, predict that, by the year 2000,

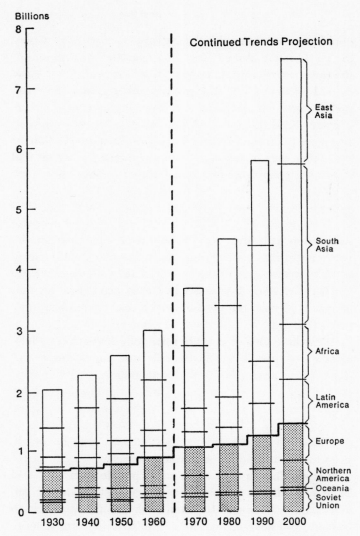

FIGURE 3. Numerical Growth of World Population, 1930–2000. The great disparity in numbers of people between the developed and developing nations will become much greater in the next thirty-five years if present trends continue.

SOURCE: Population Reference Bureau, *Population Bulletin* (October 1965), p. 80.

population in these developing areas will have tripled to 5.4 billion. As Figure 3 shows, the population of the three less developed continents will increase during the second half of this century by a number greater than the present world population.

It required, then, all the thousands of years of his residence on earth for man to grow to a population of more than 3 billion. Yet, at present rates, this figure will more than double in the next thirty-five years (see Figure 4).

For the world as a whole, not only have the total numbers increased, but also the annual rates of increase have risen steadily. For 1750 it is estimated that the rate of growth was 0.29 per cent per year. A century later that rate had nearly doubled to 0.51 per cent annually. In 1960 it was 1.8 per cent per year. At this rate the population of the world doubles in less than forty years.

After thousands of years of relatively slow growth in the number of people in the world, how did science suddenly bring about this explosive increase?

Why Are They Here?

Almost all of this tremendous increase can be attributed to applications of scientific research.

It is possible to feed many more people than we could have kept alive a century or two ago. Plant and animal stocks have been greatly improved through research in biology, physiology, and soil chemistry. Stronger, more fruitful hybrid plants and animals supply more and better food. The application of commercial fertilizers and power

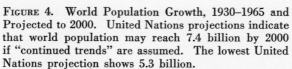

Billions

World Population:

The Past 35 Years... | The Next 35 Years

A

B

C

UN Projections:

A   Continued Trends

B   Medium

C   Low

1930   1965   2000

FIGURE 4. World Population Growth, 1930–1965 and Projected to 2000. United Nations projections indicate that world population may reach 7.4 billion by 2000 if "continued trends" are assumed. The lowest United Nations projection shows 5.3 billion.

SOURCE: Population Reference Bureau, *Population Bulletin* (October 1965), p. 77.

machinery to farming has increased the production of foodstuffs enormously. Not only food, but also fibers and building materials for providing clothing and shelter can be distributed quickly and easily as a result of scientific and technological advances in transportation and communication.

But far more important in explaining the rate of population growth are advances in medicine. Research in chemistry, biochemistry, physiology, anatomy, and biology has led to the drastic reduction of infectious and contagious diseases, as well as to improvement in maternal care, infant care, and public sanitation. Such discoveries as pasteurization, inoculation, penicillin, sulfanilamides, and DDT have dramatically cut human death rates. And virtually all the recent increases in the world's population are the result of reductions in the death rate, not of rises in the birth rate—which is precisely why the rates of growth are so unevenly distributed in the world today.

The rates of increase show considerable variation among countries and world regions. The most striking differences are those between highly industrialized regions and underdeveloped regions that have not experienced an industrial revolution. Most of the countries of northwestern Europe seem to be approaching a relatively stable population. In those countries the decline in rates of population growth was associated with rapid industrialization, which began about 1760. Today, interestingly enough, it is the underdeveloped areas that have shown the most striking increases in rates of growth.

Unlike northwestern Europe in the nineteenth century, when industrialization and improvement in medicine went hand in hand, many present-day underdeveloped areas

have reaped some of the benefits of modern medical care
without at the same time becoming industrialized. In
other words, we have the diffusion of one set of cultural
patterns—scientific medical care—without the spread of
a second set of patterns that historically had been associated with the first. In fact, the application of medicine
in cutting the death rate—without, however, cutting the
birth rate—has produced a decline in mortality rates
much sharper than any ever experienced in the history of
the presently industrialized nations.

This striking cut in the death rates in underdeveloped
areas has been accomplished by international programs
of disease control rather than as a consequence of economic development in the areas themselves. The decrease
in the death rate, therefore, does not require and has not
been accompanied by parallel changes in values, customs,
or culture patterns. It does not, as it did in the Western
world, imply any significant growth of per capita income
or increase in the level of general education. In short,
the reduction of the death rates in Asia, Africa, and Latin
America is not accompanied by the kinds of basic social
change that also lead to declining birth rates: education,
industrialization, urbanization, and the emergence of a
consumer-oriented middle class.

Because disease control in nonindustrial countries has
not occurred along with alterations in income, education,
and social values, the birth rate has remained high. Even
though the odds now are that all his children will live, a
man still has many children just as he did in the days
when several of them probably would have died in infancy. Each of his sons is capable of fathering another
large family; each of his daughters is capable of bearing

as many children as her own mother bore. It is this continuing high birth rate combined with a sharply reduced death rate that accounts for the population explosion.

The nations that are now industrialized began lowering their birth rates before their death rates declined sharply, but the underdeveloped areas will not experience declining birth rates until long after their death rates have reached the low levels characteristic of industrial societies. Therefore, the poorest and most densely populated countries of the world are the very ones producing people at rates they cannot afford. Their fantastic population growth does not reflect increasing national strength, social progress, or economic development. On the contrary, population increase for these countries impedes the possibility of economic development, rising levels of income, and increasing educational opportunities.

Kingsley Davis and Philip M. Hauser, widely respected social scientists and students of population, both doubt that economic development can even keep pace with the rate of population increase in these areas, much less exceed it enough to raise the standard of living. In the face of world-wide demand for improved levels of living, a "revolution of rising expectations," current rates of population increase make lowered levels of living seem more likely. If this proves to be the case, it raises the question of how long the industrialized nations can maintain their relatively luxurious way of life while surrounded by people living in ever-more-miserable poverty.

Within this context, let us look at trends in the United States, not only in replacement of personnel, but also in the distribution of population by age, sex, and location.

American Trends

The population of the United States grows by one person every 10.5 seconds. Our rate of increase is about the same as the world average, 1.8 per cent per year—extremely high for an industrialized nation. But perhaps the most significant trend in the American population is not the growth rate as such, but a change in the distribution of the population.

Social scientists estimate that over half of the population increase between 1960 and 1970 will occur among people under eighteen and over sixty-five. The relative growth of the group that constitutes the bulk of the labor force, people between twenty-one and sixty-five years of age, will be less than that of the population as a whole. Indeed, not only the proportion, but also the actual number of those aged thirty-five to forty-four will decline slightly. In other words, our population will be about one-sixth larger in 1970 than it was in 1960, but it will also be different in composition: There will be more people under twenty-one and more people over sixty-five. This shift means many more dependents or, to put it another way, a relatively smaller labor force to accomplish a larger job.

The population projection for 1970 estimates 114 million Americans between seventeen and sixty-five, but 75 million under eighteen and 20 million over sixty-five. For heads of families sixty-five or older, median income in 1959 was $1,840, as contrasted with $5,730 for breadwinners between thirty-five and forty-four years old. But the burden on the people active in the labor force will be even greater than these figures suggest, for an increasing proportion of the older people will be women. During the present decade, we are adding nearly two women to the over-sixty-five group for every man, and many of those women are widows.

There are, of course, regional variations in these trends. Throughout American history there has been a long-term pattern of two streams of migration: from south to north and from east to west. Although the rural South has a relatively high birth rate, its proportion of the national population declines as southerners move north and west. As Hauser says, the North and West are the productive parts of the United States, and the South is the reproductive part. These trends will no doubt continue for some time. The Southwest, the Mountain and Pacific Coast states, Alaska, and Hawaii will gain population faster than the national average. (So will Florida, an exception to the general situation in the South.)

Migration also causes regional variations in the age distribution of the population. For example, the population of the Pacific Coast states will increase about 80 per cent between 1950 and 1970 and will increase its labor force by almost two-thirds, whereas New England's population will grow 20 per cent in the same period, but its working population will increase by only 5 per cent.

The rural population will continue to become a smaller proportion of the total. When we count our 30 million new Americans in the 1970 census, 25 million of them will be in metropolitan areas. Many central cities will continue to grow more slowly than the rest of the country, but by 1970 two-thirds of all Americans will live in metropolitan areas (including suburbs).

What is a tide of teen-agers in the 1960s will become a

flood of young adults in the 1970s. We expect, therefore, a high marriage rate in the next decade. It is appropriate, then, to examine the structure of the American family and to identify those social trends that are shaping its future.

The Family and Reproduction

Throughout human history, the family has been the core social group. It has been into the family that children have been born, and, for that matter, it has been the center of all the other activities essential to the survival of society. In most societies, the family has served as the matrix of economic life, producing and distributing most of its own goods and services. Children have been taught the skills they need to participate in their society, not by hired teachers, but by relatives. Even today, in small, relatively isolated societies, the family is the basic primary group around which the major tasks of social life are organized.

In all societies, ancient or modern, small or large, the family is the structure that provides for the reproduction of almost all new members of the society. Families may be organized with one husband, one wife, and their children; or one husband, multiple wives, and their children; or one wife, multiple husbands, and their children. Or they may consist of great-grandparents plus all their male children and spouses for four generations. And so on. Regardless of the kind of family and kinship organization called for by the culture, all societies have some family structure, and it is within that structure that reproduction customarily occurs.

The sexual life of man is not confined to the marriage situation, but all societies have rules attempting to guarantee that reproduction will take place within a family framework. Everywhere there are variations in premarital relations, and various extramarital patterns may be permitted along with more formalized family life.

In some tribes, prenuptial intercourse is not only permitted but even expected, but there is no evidence of complete promiscuity in any society. Everywhere the incest taboos and kinship, age, and class rules limit the relations of the sexes both before and after marriage. Although many peoples encourage, or at least tolerate, premarital relations, such relations generally are considered preparatory to marriage.

There is no uniformity in attitudes about permissive premarital relations. In contiguous tribes, for instance, one group may put a high value on chastity, whereas neighboring groups may consider it of no consequence at all. Some folk societies, such as the Veddahs and other Negrito peoples, have strong taboos against prenuptial sexual relations, as has our own society, in which chastity is at least an "official" virtue.

A study by Julia Brown of 110 nonliterate societies around the world reveals that the least frequently and most lightly punished deviation from the sexual mores is premarital sexual relations, especially when the partners are betrothed. The offenses most frequently and severely punished are incest, abduction, and rape. Furthermore, the punishment increases with the likelihood of the offender's causing a child to be born outside the familial structure. As a pregnancy arising from premarital sexual relations is likely to be followed by marriage, such relations are less severely punished than is rape. In Western societies, the mother of an illegitimate child is often scorned, and the child may be denied the right of inheritance. In all societies, sets of sanctions encourage the confinement of reproduction to the family.

The Changing Role of the Family

Present-day American family life reveals changes in the relations of parents and children that have grown out of current economic trends. In urban communities particularly, the absence of the father from home for long hours leaves to the mother nearly all duties of child training and discipline, a condition not present in the earlier American family.

In pioneer and early rural America, the husband and wife shared most economic functions. The household was the center of many work activities in which the wife played a definite role. Spinning, weaving, and making clothes continued for a long time to be her duties, and, even after machine industry had replaced a great deal of home manufacture, she continued to make the clothes for the family. Then, too, she took charge of curing meat, of preserving vegetables and fruit for winter use, and usually of providing the milk, eggs, and garden produce. The household members were concerned with making a living rather than with earning wages.

Today the family is less and less a producing and consuming unit, especially in urban localities. Among farm families some of the older patterns remain, but the commercialization and mechanization of agriculture are dissolving the older rural, home-centered economy.

When reproduction and care of offspring are the central purposes of family life, the child is often considered an economic asset. Among peasant peoples everywhere, children are put to work at early ages in the fields and in the household. Even in some preagricultural societies boys are initiated early into fishing and hunting activities and girls into household duties. Today in the more industrialized societies, child labor has pretty well disappeared.

It is easy to overemphasize the importance of the reproductive function in societal continuity and to overlook the fact that the familial structure also has functions for the many married couples who are childless. Some couples never have children; others live together for years before having children. In a society characterized by conjugal families, many couples live together for years after their children have left to found households of their own.

A strong need for security is present in every human being. It is built up in the child within the structure of the family. Adults carry over into later life this same need for reassurance and emotional support from others. Today, with fewer children per family and with the disappearance of economic and educational activities from the home, husbands and wives are more and more dependent on companionship and sexual attraction to keep them together.

Sexual relations, childbearing, and child rearing have proportionately a much larger place in total family life than they once had. In contrast, the family is no longer a relatively self-sufficient food-, clothing-, and shelter-producing organization. The members of the family do not work together as a unit for purposes of production and distribution of goods and services. The economic functions of the family and the home have become steadily less important. Comparable changes have occurred in other familial functions: religious and occupational training, for example.

Marriage Trends in the United States

In spite of some popular notions about the ill effects of divorce and the emancipation of women on the American family generally, not only is a high proportion of our population married—the highest in our history—but also our young people wed at relatively early ages. In fact, the average marriage age has been dropping for some decades. The median age at first marriage for men declined from 26.1 years in 1890 to 23.1 in 1964; the corresponding figures for women were 22.0 and 20.5.

Though the marriage rate has been high, the average size of the American family has been declining. At the time of our first census in 1790, the average number of persons per family was 5.7. A hundred years later it was 4.9. By 1940 it had fallen to 3.8 and by 1960 to 3.6. The changes in family size are correlated with (1) increases in childless marriage, the extent of which is attested by the fact that 15 per cent of American women who marry bear no children; (2) an aging population, which means that more families with no minor children survive than formerly; and (3) the increase in the average time span between marriage and birth of the first child.

The decline in the average size of the individual family should not lead us to lose sight of the fact that, with the lowered death rate, the American population, like that of the world, is increasing—and increasing rapidly. Businessmen looking for markets or politicians who equate size with strength sometimes view our expanding population with unalloyed glee. But population growth brings population problems. Much of our increase is in households headed by very young people or by widows or retired men—which means smaller households with smaller incomes. The proportional reduction in the labor force is evidence that population growth does not necessarily mean increased national productive capacity.

A Crucial Question for Americans

How can we reduce the rate of population increase in the United States and in the world?

The question is not whether to reduce the rate of population growth, but how. Mankind cannot survive indefinitely the present explosive rate of increase. Even with our enormous wealth of natural resources and our astonishing productive capacity, the United States cannot long sustain its way of life if its population doubles every forty years.

No one can predict population accurately, and social scientists know it. But we can project arithmetically what population will be if it continues to grow at its present rate. The reason we cannot *predict* what will happen is that man is capable of altering his own behavior. Human beings have affected the environment in which they live so that they are not mere subjects of the biological laws of evolution. Man is a culture-creating, culture-bearing, and culture-transmitting animal. He can take some of his environment with him wherever he goes, and he can alter his surroundings. He can bring heat to the Arctic and refrigeration to the tropics. Because man can, in some

46

measure, change the world in which he lives (he does not simply respond to it), he has affected his own reproductive cycle. The death rate in Ceylon, for example, was cut 50 per cent in less than ten years by antibiotics and DDT. It is naïve to say that man should not interfere with his natural rate of population growth; he has already done so on a rather mammoth scale. Through a deliberate policy of applying scientific knowledge, man has changed the pattern of human death rates. By the same means, he can alter human birth rates.

Two powerful ideologies oppose birth control: Marxism and Roman Catholicism. The reasons, of course, are quite different. Both Communist and non-Communist Marxists are committed to the dogma that birth control is a capitalist strategy for subduing and exploiting the colonial masses. Doctrinaire Marxists contend that overpopulation is not possible in a society in which the worker is not separated from the means of production and in which the wealth is equitably distributed. Even within the Communist camp, however, there has been pressure to reinterpret the Marxist position. The several Communist nations have taken various positions on this doctrine. China has vacillated. The government enthusiastically backed a program of birth control, mounting a nationwide educational campaign in 1956–1957. Then, during the Great Leap Forward, orthodoxy returned, and Malthus was seen as irreconcilable with Marx. At present, birth control is again being frankly advocated in China, with diagrams and devices on display.

The Catholic Church, on the other hand, although disapproving of mechanical and chemical methods of avoiding conception, admits the problem of overpopulation.

Pope Pius XII recognized the desirability of population control for economic and social reasons. But to achieve what it calls "responsible parenthood," the Church approves only such methods as delayed marriage, abstinence, and the "rhythm method" of contraception—techniques that are probably inadequate to the magnitude of the task in underdeveloped areas. One should note, of course, that —as in the various Communist nations—different social classes and ethnic groups among Catholics evidence varying degrees of orthodoxy in practicing the tenets of their ideology.

Both the Catholic and the Communist positions are significant because they affect international policy, but their impact should not be overestimated. The core of the problem is the fact that most people in the underdeveloped areas do not recognize rapid population growth as a problem. They not only lack effective means of controlling fertility; they also have no desire to inhibit uncontrolled birth rates because they have no awareness of overpopulation as a problem.

We who recognize the trend and its potential consequences have so far refused to share our knowledge of impending disaster with those most concerned. Former President Eisenhower has said that "birth control is no business of the United States government." We have made the reduction of deaths our "business." To abdicate responsibility for the corollary reduction of births is sheer irresponsibility.

The United States government has spent enormous sums of money to lower the death rates not only of Americans but also of people all around the world. The efficient health agencies that we finance have exported reduced death rates so effectively that we have, to some extent, created the population explosion.

Whereas annual per capita income in the United States approaches $2,000, more than two-thirds of the countries in the world still have per capita incomes of less than $400 a year. As we have pointed out, these countries are exactly the ones in which death rates have been falling rapidly and birth rates have remained high. If an economy grows while the size of the population remains constant, then the increase raises the average level of living. But even a growing economy can be outstripped by an increasing population. Indeed, when population grows faster than per capita income, the reduced level of living may itself impede further economic growth. That is, severe poverty will make it difficult to increase the amount of education, will leave little capital free for investment, and may well lead to political instability that will discourage the investment of foreign capital.

Research by Edward G. Stockwell of the U. S. Bureau of the Census suggests a definite relationship between population growth and economic development. He computed the average annual percentage change in per capita income between 1952 and 1958 for sixteen underdeveloped nations and related these changes to the annual rates of population growth during the same period. The annual rate of increase in per capita income tended to be inversely proportional to the rate of population growth. That is, those countries that experienced the highest annual rates of population growth realized, with few exceptions, the smallest gains in per capita income. In the polar cases, Austria had a population growth rate of 0.2 and a per capita income growth rate of 7.2, while Ecuador, with an annual rate of population increase of 3.3, achieved a rate of growth in per capita income of only 0.8.

For those countries whose population grew at rates of less than 1 per cent per year, the annual rate of increase in per capita income ranged from 3.1 to 7.5 per cent, with an average rate of 5.9 per cent per year. The rate of per capita income growth was only 2.4 per cent in countries whose population increase was between 1 and 2 per cent, and it was only 1.7 per cent in those countries where population increase was more than 2 per cent per year. In other words, most countries with population growth rates of more than 2 per cent per year are not experiencing enough economic growth to stay even: Their per capita income is dropping year by year despite their economic achievements.

It seems clear that rapid population increases exert serious retarding effects on the economies of underdeveloped countries. It is an oversimplification, however, to so emphasize population growth that we ignore the importance of technology. Ultimately, the wealth of nations is determined by the technology that they are able to bring to bear, for it is the machinery of mass production that greatly increases productivity and reduces the cost of living.

To earn enough money to buy a pound of fish, for example, requires 19 minutes of labor in the United States. In Great Britain it requires 23 minutes of labor, in the Soviet Union 170, in India 216, and in China 300. We can hardly attribute these differences directly to the pressure of population, for Great Britain is much more densely populated than either India or China, and the United States is more densely populated than the Soviet Union. But the

United States and Great Britain enjoy the fruits of a much higher level of technological development than the other three countries. In 1951, William F. Ogburn used as an index of technological development the annual per capita consumption of energy of all kinds expressed in hundreds of kilowatt hours. The energy consumption figures for the five countries were United States, 130; United Kingdom, 71; Soviet Union, 22; India, 4; and China, 2. What is being achieved through scientific technology using mechanical energy in the United States is being accomplished by human energy in China. The latter method is much more expensive in man-hours; hence the difference in the minutes of labor required to buy fish (or most other things) in the industrial and nonindustrial societies.

It is not population density as such, then, but the lack of technological development that accounts for such striking differences in levels of living. The significance of the population explosion in underdeveloped nations is that the expanding population consumes the wealth that might otherwise be channeled into technological development. Countries whose main item of production is more human beings seem doomed to use those human beings as sources of energy, for their population production leaves them unable to afford the machines that purchase leisure.

The notion that economic problems associated with population expansion are confined to technologically backward societies is comfortable, but misleading. Iceland, for example, was a poor rural society, which became modern in the span of a generation. But its population growth rate is eating up the profits. From 1950 to 1960, the average annual rate of growth in Iceland's gross national product was 4.1 per cent, nearly as high as the average for European member countries of the Organization for Economic Cooperation and Development during the same period. Icleand's rate of population growth, however, remains so much higher than in the other countries that its *per capita* economic increase is the lowest in the OECD.

There is another dangerous illusion: that we can solve the problem of population growth in the United States and ignore the situation in the rest of the world. Latin America, for instance, would have to double its agricultural and industrial production within thirty years merely to remain at its present low level of living. And more and more Latin Americans are dissatisfied with that level of living. Should we not help them to understand the part that population growth plays in the economic equation? Should we wait for them to direct their frustrations and hostilities toward their prosperous neighbor to the north? We cannot survive indefinitely as hostages on an island of plenty in a sea of poverty.

CHAPTER 4

Education for What?
American Traits and Trends

Even more dramatic than the growth of population is the increase in the amount of formal education taken for granted by Americans.

At the turn of the century, the average American left school at twelve or thirteen years of age, having completed the elementary grades. By 1930, the average American youth was staying in school until he was fifteen or sixteen years old. By 1960, 80 per cent of our young people were being graduated from high school, and one of every two high-school graduates was going on to college. As Figure 5 shows, while more than doubling the number of high-school graduates between 1940 and 1965, we more than tripled the number who went on to college.

**In 1965 54% of high-school graduates went
on to college compared with 34% in 1940.**

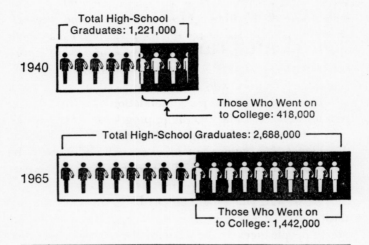

FIGURE 5. Number of High-School Graduates in the
United States Going on to College, 1940–1965
SOURCE: *The New York Times*, March 20, 1966, p. E13.
© 1966 by The New York Times Company. Reprinted by
permission.

A college education is no longer considered merely
polish for an elite minority. Among the younger generation, it is very nearly a requirement for a middle-class
member of the labor force. It is likely to become more so
as the impact of automation is felt.

Automation, which George Meany of the AFL-CIO has
called "The Second Industrial Revolution," cuts the need

for some kinds of workers in the labor force, but it increases the need for others. We have less and less need for unskilled laborers. In 1960, 460,000 production workers produced more steel than 540,000 had produced in 1950. Where unemployment rates are high, the ranks of the jobless are filled with displaced production-line workers. "Retraining" is by no means the panacea that it may seem at first glance. What we need are more and more white-collar workers, minor managers, professionals, and executives. The very workers first displaced by automation are those with an inadequate foundation of formal education on which to build retraining programs.

The technological changes brought about by scientific discoveries and engineering advances will undoubtedly be translated, in the long run, into shorter work hours, higher incomes, and less drudgery. But, as Lord Keynes pointed out, in the long run we are all dead. In the short run, we must face the question of how to handle the 1,350,000 young people entering the job market each year, more than half of them with only high-school education or less.

Social science certainly does not have all the answers, but a good start on the road to useful answers can be made by asking the right questions. This chapter considers what we are doing in the field of education and to whom we are doing it. We shall turn in the next chapter to a discussion of trends in the American labor force and economy.

The Changing Role of the Family in Education

The crucial early learning experiences of a child, as we noted in the previous chapter, normally take place in the family. His enthusiasm for learning, his attitudes toward new experience, his whole approach to later, more formal, education are shaped, intentionally or unintentionally, by his family. Some of the things he learns are deliberately and consciously taught by his parents, older siblings, and other close relatives. The child also learns a great deal "nondeliberately"—that is, unconsciously—especially basic attitudes and values.

The home also provides the first recreational patterns for the child, though play groups furnish important connections with the wider world outside. In earlier times the family frequently participated as a unit in recreation: in games, picnics, family reunions. Today the individualized nature of recreation has tended to remove this function almost entirely from the home, although radio, television, and the automobile have done something to reunite the family in leisure activities.

As for education, the family provides the bases of all the child's later formal learning. The interaction of parents and children is the foundation upon which most of the intellectual and emotional conditioning of the latter takes place. In earlier societies the home furnished much of what is now part of formal education; and, in spite of great changes, the family still gives the child his basic training in the social attitudes and habits important to adult participation in social life. Habits of bodily care, of social relations, and of managing the material world are learned in interaction with one's parents.

But one consequence of the Industrial Revolution is that, although mothers and fathers still provide models for much behavior, children no longer learn the norms of work as they once did in the family. The separation of place of work from place of residence (a consequence of the requirements of the mass-production line) removes working fathers from the view of their children. Even in the English textile mills in the early days of the Industrial Revolution, when workers and their families lived beneath the factory roof, children learned to spin and weave from their parents. But the boy who helped his father on the farm now has a grandson majoring in soil chemistry at Iowa State.

In most societies throughout most of human history the father did not go to work, because work was in or adjacent to his home. The reason he goes to work now is that he is a specialist who contributes his knowledge or his acquired skill to making one part of one part of a product. Few people in our labor force can point to a finished product and say, "I made that." So the father's skill can be used only on an assembly line, whether it is a production or an intellectual-staff line, and he has to go join other men in a work environment, separated from their places of residence, where they can pool their skills. Most children thus do not see their fathers earning a living.

Contrast this pattern with that of a nonindustrial society in which the men get up every morning and go out to fish and the women get up and garden. What happens to little boys and little girls in such a society? They play until they are four or five years old, as little boys and girls should. When a boy is about six years old, he starts going out on the boat with his father and his uncles as a general handyman. He gets in the way, as six-year-old boys will, but he helps a little too. He can hand them this or that, and he watches what is going on. By the time he is eight years old, he knows enough to help mend nets. By the time he is ten, he is beginning to learn where the good fishing spots are and to be able to tell what kind of weather is good for fishing. At twelve he not only knows how to repair his father's boat, but he has worked on it enough to know how to build one himself. At about fourteen he goes through a ceremony at the end of which he is told, "You are now a man!" He is ready to get on the boat the next morning and go to work with the other adults. He doesn't have to be sent to a naval college; he doesn't take any courses in bait-cutting. He already knows the job. He has been living with it for years.

His little sister, meanwhile, helps to sweep the hearth when she is seven. She helps to grind the maize by the time she is nine and to prepare food by the time she is twelve. She knows about planting seasons and harvesting seasons. By the time she is fourteen and old enough to marry, she is long past the need for a course in home economics. She has had that course at home.

This type of training is very rare in our society. Most American children have very little idea of what their fathers do when they go to work: Fathers go and they come home. Furthermore, many wives are unaware of the exact nature of their husbands' jobs. When sociological research involves interviews in a district where factory workers live, it is not at all unusual to record conversation between interviewer and housewife of the following kind:

"What does your husband do?"

"He's at the Ford plant."

"What does he do there?"

"He works over at the Ford plant—you know."

"Is he on the assembly line, is he a machine operator, is he a supply man?"

"I don't know. He's worked over at the Ford plant for ten years now."

Under such circumstances, one can hardly expect the youth in a specialized economy to be able to move out of adolescence into an adult occupational role without difficulty; he has had no chance to learn how to be an adult member of the labor force through practice or through imitation.

Americans place a tremendous burden on their formal educational system. As responsibilities are gradually removed from the realm of the family, we ask the school to take them over. Public schools are expected by many citizens to teach children discipline, to be responsible for their moral training and guidance, and even to organize their recreation. When a fifteen-year-old tough creates a disturbance in a downtown department store on a Monday morning, the first reaction of clerks and shoppers—and you and me—is apt to be, "Why isn't that kid in school?" Later, if at all, we wonder why he isn't in a psychiatrist's office or in jail. Few of us ask why his parents don't know where he is or why they didn't do a better job of rearing him.

That the people of the United States put great stress on education is suggested by the following figures: The enrollment in schools and colleges in 1960 was more than 46 million individuals. The full-time enrollees in 1947 accounted for 42 per cent of all individuals between five and thirty-four years old; by 1960 the figure had risen to 56 per cent. Of all American children between the ages of seven and fourteen, more than 99 out of 100 were in school. In no other country in the world and at no other time in history has such a large proportion of a population been in school.

School opportunities have been constantly expanding

for some decades. In 1880, of the 15 million individuals aged five to seventeen years in our population, fewer than two-thirds were enrolled in school. By 1947, 85 per cent, and by 1960 more than 90 per cent, of this age group were in school. By 1900 compulsory elementary education had become firmly established. And, although secondary-school enrollments had been going up slowly since 1880, after 1910 they increased rapidly. In 1890 there were about 400,000 high-school students; in 1910 about 900,-000. In 1940 there were 6.6 million; by 1960 there were more than 10.2 million. The growth of college and university enrollments has also been impressive. In 1900 there were only about 200,000 students in this category. The next forty years saw a million added to this number. In 1950 there were more than 2.2 million students in American colleges and universities; and in 1960 college and university enrollments reached a record high of more than 3.5 million. Figure 6 shows that educational enrollment in the United States has increased by more than 30 per cent in a decade. Between 1940 and 1964 we nearly doubled the proportion of high-school and college graduates in the labor force. Social scientists at the U. S. Bureau of the Census predict a total school enrollment, through college, of more than 60 million by 1970.

Despite the constantly mounting pressure of numbers, the quality of education in the United States remains high. Not long ago it was fashionable for adults to lament the fact that "youngsters nowadays don't learn as much as they did when I went to school." (Perhaps some oldsters attributed this decline to a softness in curriculum accompanying the abolition of the two-mile walk through the snow, which was a standard feature of grandparental

**Enrollment in elementary, secondary and higher education
has increased by 31% in ten years.**

1956-1957

Elementary and Secondary   Higher Education
39.5 Million   3.1 Million

Total:
42.6 Million

1966-1967

Elementary and Secondary   Higher Education
49.9 Million   5.9 Million

Total:
55.8 Million

**The number of degrees conferred by higher institutions
has risen by 77%.**

1956-1957

409,000
Degrees

1966-1967

722,000
Degrees

**And total spending for all fields of learning in the U.S.
has grown by 124%.**

1956-1957

$21.8
Billion

1966-1967

$48.8
Billion

FIGURE 6. Our Rapidly Expanding Educational System
SOURCE: *The New York Times*, September 4, 1966, p. E9.
© 1966 by The New York Times Company. Reprinted by
permission.

educational recollections.) Undoubtedly many people felt that traditional learning was being neglected for frills as they watched the impact of rapid social change on the school system.

During the present century, the main shift in elementary and secondary education has been from curricula oriented to subject matter to an emphasis upon the child as a growing personality. Under the former, most weight was given to content and capacity to reproduce what had been read or heard. Today the school is more and more child-centered, with stress on the self and on social development.

In the matter of method, the change has been from a rather severe, authoritarian to a more permissive practice, in which the child has a larger degree of participation. "Progressive education," though now largely discarded as a formal technique, has influenced even the more conservative public and parochial schools. Matters of motivation, cooperative learning, and mental hygiene are given much attention.

The rapid rise in high-school population, especially after 1910, led to a proliferation of separate courses and to such varied courses of study as liberal or college-preparatory, commercial, vocational, and fine arts. The drift has been away from courses designed to prepare the pupil for higher education toward those that have more practical usefulness in jobs or in the home and that give the future citizen some orientation to his public and political rights and duties. The ancient languages, algebra, geometry, trigonometry, and formal political history have tended to give way to modern languages, simplified "unified" mathematics, and social studies with emphasis on current problems. Intense competition with the Soviet Union, however, has led to a re-examination of the desirability of a stronger emphasis on science and mathematics. It was argued in many high quarters of government and education that the Russian superiority or success arose from far more thorough training in the natural sciences, mathematics, and technology than that offered in the United States.

Nonetheless, research evidence suggests that children acquire as much skill in traditional subjects today as they did a generation ago. Despite time devoted to student "government," driver education, and current affairs, tests given to eleventh-grade students in subjects like mathematics show that nowadays youngsters know as much as or more than scholars tested in the same subjects at the same schools thirty years ago.

Anything less would be unfortunate—there is a great deal more to learn today than there was thirty years ago. In a primitive society, an individual may possess a considerable amount of detailed information. Perhaps an Australian aborigine knows as much about kinship structure as a Swiss watchmaker knows about clocks. A Bushman may have as large a fund of information about tracking game as an econometrician has about game theory. But most of what that one Bushman knows all the adult male members of his tribe also know. In a society in which occupations are relatively undifferentiated, the occupational lore of one man is about the same information that everyone else has. To oversimplify slightly, in a society in which all women garden and cook and all men hunt and fish, the total content of the culture is not a lot more complicated than the knowledge of any two adults of opposite sexes.

Two consequences of the growth of science and technology are elaborate occupational specialization and an increase in the content of culture. Bushmen do not have much more to transmit than one Bushman can know. Americans have so much more shared, learned behavior to transmit than one American could know that the task of organizing a program of general education becomes staggering.

In the school, changes are taking place that are very similar to the continuing changes in the family. The school is an important factor in teaching, of course, but the trend seems to be away from its serving as a finishing school in *occupational* learning. Many older lawyers tell us that they *really* learned their profession in their postgraduate stints as clerks in law firms. What happens to the boy who is graduated from the shop curriculum in a technical high school? He becomes, not a welder, but a welder's apprentice on a construction project. Often we praise corporations that encourage students to get a broad general educational base and let the company teach them the details of the job. We laud such firms for their enlightened dedication to the liberal arts, when their actual motivation is anchored in the quite rational assumption that, given the complicated network of social expectations engendered by pooling the skills of specialists in a complex organization, the agency best equipped to train one to fit into that network is that organization.

There is more to the debate of educational policy, of course, than the question of how vocationally oriented a curriculum should be. Fundamentally, this question drives us back to the philosophical differences between the so-called "rationalists" on the one hand and the "relativists" on the other. The rationalist assumes that there is a set of fixed universal truths or absolutes about human nature. As Robert Maynard Hutchins says:

> One purpose of education is to draw out the common elements of our human nature. These elements are the same in any time or place. The notion of educating a man to live in a particular time or place, to adjust him to any particular environment, is therefore foreign to a true conception of education.
>
> Education implies teaching. Teaching implies knowledge. Knowledge is truth. The truth is everywhere the same. Hence education should be everywhere the same.

Rationalists like Hutchins place relatively little emphasis on science as a means for understanding human behavior. They would organize education around the great works of literature and philosophy. The relativists, in contrast, consider science the greatest single tool for the understanding of man and the universe. For them there are no absolutes in human behavior; they view culture from a relativistic standpoint, as an ever-changing set of ideas and values. But both the relativist disciples of Dewey and their opponents who follow Hutchins and Adler must be concerned with the problem of the survival of their society in the age of science.

Education as Social Policy

How can an educational system meet the challenge of the social products of scientific technology? Can our economy support an atmosphere of free inquiry? Can our schools staff an occupationally specialized economy?

These questions lead some people to despair. John

Fischer of *Harper's,* for example, suggests that, in a technologically oriented economy, the 22 per cent of our population with I.Q.s below 89 may never learn to do any useful
job. As he points out, in industrialized countries, human
muscle has become almost obsolete: Anything it can lift,
a machine can lift better. Any task involving repetition
of the same motions can be done more rapidly and less
expensively by mechanical or electronic devices.

Certainly there is some evidence that our educational
and economic problems intersect in the one-fifth of our
population that is well below average in intelligence. The
Bureau of Labor Statistics reports that 80 per cent of the
youngsters who drop out of school are lagging by at least
one grade. The psychologist Lee J. Cronbach argues that,
by the end of high school, almost no one with an I.Q.
below 85 is still in school. This problem, coupled with
the requirement for specialized occupational training, is
undoubtedly one reason why the unemployment rate for
sixteen-to-nineteen-year-olds is twice as high as it is for
adults.

But it is dangerous to overestimate the accuracy of I.Q.
tests. Although they do measure native ability, at least
roughly, the measurement is warped to some extent by
the test-taker's learned motivation to perform well on tests
and by the opportunities he has had to acquire certain facts
and practice certain kinds of reasoning. Ordinary Stanford-Binet I.Q. tests exaggerate the innate brainpower of
people who come from comfortable middle-class backgrounds and underestimate the intelligence of those from
culturally deprived farm or laboring-class environments.

A person's class status, with its concomitant income, education, and style of life, greatly affects the likelihood that

certain things will happen to him. Position in the class structure greatly influences many of life's chances: the chance to stay alive during the first year after birth, the opportunity to view fine art, the chance to remain healthy and grow tall and to recover from illness quickly, the chance to avoid becoming a juvenile delinquent, and— very crucially—the chance to complete intermediate or higher education. It is easy to dismiss many failures arising from limited life chances with the notion that the individual controls his own destiny; the observation, for instance, that class status influences one's opportunities to view fine art can be brushed aside with the retort that museums are free and that, if a person doesn't take advantage of them, it is his own fault. Such a view fails to take into account the power of subculture. A child reared in a slum area who does not even know of the existence of museums or who has learned to believe that painting is for "sissies" or "squares" has different chances for art experience than does one brought up in a middle-class home and taught that all educated people know something about art.

Recent sociological and psychological research suggests that a person's I.Q. is by no means a fixed entity. Apparently, an increase in motivation coupled with special instruction can raise an individual's I.Q. by several points. It follows that, in an intellectually stifling environment, a person can grow progressively duller—a suspicion many of us have entertained after a poor choice of vacation spots.

In addition, the research of Jacob W. Getzels and Philip W. Jackson at the University of Chicago indicates that I.Q. tests effectively measure ability to deal with numbers and language but that they fail to measure capacity to cope with sounds, shapes, colors, and social relationships. In other words, we may, in relying on these tests, be defining intelligence in such a way as to exclude what we usually call "creativity." Perhaps the most disturbing of these research findings is that teachers are likely to reward conforming pupils with high I.Q.s and to punish creative eccentrics, because the latter are more trouble.

In the United States, classroom performance is influenced by the persistence of a deep-seated cultural belief that instruction will wipe out individual differences in native ability. In spite of the laboratory, the workshop, and the project method, the printed page still holds the center of the educational stage. As a result it has been difficult to introduce novel methods of instruction into the classroom and to break the hold of traditional teacher-pupil relations on the learning process. Yet considerable advances have been made in the recognition of individual differences in learning ability, for example, by provision of separate classes for fast, medium, and slow learners and by training teachers in day-to-day awareness of such differences.

But we make it exceedingly difficult for the public-school teacher to help each child reach his potential. (There is no doubt that, for most people, education stops far short of their capacities for self-development. I.Q. scores of a sample of draftees show that the brightest teamster is smarter than the average physician, whereas the lowest scores of professionals fall below the averages for manual laborers.) Americans are uneasy about giving special attention to especially talented children. On one hand, they tend to confuse the ideal of democracy with an ethic of equalitarianism. A recent public-opinion poll indicates that 80 per cent of Americans believe that teachers should give extra help to dull students, whereas only 20 per cent believe it to be proper for above-average pupils to receive extra attention. If the assumption is made that exceptional ability or outstanding achievement is somehow undemocratic, then our educational system probably will be geared to the lowest common denominator. On the other hand, precisely because our economy is not an equalitarian one, we fall a long way short of actually providing equality of opportunity. As Fischer says:

Wealthier parents, quite naturally, try hard to protect their duller offspring from the consequences of their stupidity. As a result, prosperous communities are likely to spend an inordinate amount of their school money trying to cosset and prop up the mental laggards—to the neglect of the uncommonly able. At the same time, our poorer neighborhoods are likely to have poor schools, where the bright youngster may never be spotted and almost certainly will not get the intensive, top-caliber instruction he deserves.

In this social context, furthermore, the teacher is asked to be secretary, policeman, and guidance counselor, and to perform all these functions without offending either the most extreme radicals or the most vocal reactionaries in the community. The teacher assumes the role of a substitute parent in administering discipline and in exercising authority. Parents expect the teacher to assume such responsibility and frequently object when a school fails to carry out this pattern of authority. Parents are often more concerned actually with the moral and social effects of education than with formal instruction, in spite of the fact that they hold dearly to the fetish of "book learning."

A Crucial Question for Americans

How can we provide Americans with an opportunity for as much education as they can use?

Even in the United States, all men are not created equal, except in the limited sense of political rights enshrined in the Declaration of Independence and guaranteed in the Constitution. Diversity has its beauty, and, in a specialized and differentiated labor force, inequality in skills and aptitudes has its advantages.

The question here is whether or not American society capitalizes on the range of talents available in its members. When I suggest that we provide Americans with an opportunity for as much education as they can use, I do not mean "use" in any narrow pragmatic sense. Education has more uses than preparing people for occupational specialization and earning maximum incomes. Good education should help prepare a person to develop his whole self, add depth to his experiences, and bring meaning to his life.

Why does a society as rich as ours, a society with a respect for formal education approaching awe, educate its citizens at less than their capacities? When we examine the system of formal education in American society, we see that the amount and quality of education vary according to one's income, occupation, race, and region. Each of these variables has consequences, therefore, for the stratification system, not only in its own right, but to the degree that it influences educational opportunity and therefore life chances.

Not only is a low-income family hard put to finance a

college education for any of its members, but the child is also likely to quit high school in order to earn money. Family income is related not only to the amount but also to the kind of education a young person is likely to receive. Students from higher-income families can afford more education and are therefore more likely to aspire to the professions, which take years of preparation and expensive schooling. Students from families with lower incomes are more likely to enroll in commercial and industrial courses.

As we know that income and occupational prestige are positively correlated, we should expect a direct relationship between the occupational status of the parents and the amount of education given the children. Indeed there is such a relationship: The lower the occupational level of the parents, the lower the educational attainment of their children. Research at Indiana University shortly after World War II revealed that 14 per cent of the student body was composed of sons of professional men, although the latter constituted only 4 per cent of the state's population. On the other hand, only 13 per cent of the students were sons of semiskilled and unskilled laborers, although such workers made up 44 per cent of the population. This situation existed despite the fact that government aid had greatly increased the number of students from lower-class homes attending college; the G.I. Bill had nearly doubled the proportion of students from the lower occupational strata attending the university.

These occupational and income data suggest, of course, that the class structure itself has consequences for educational institutions. Studies have shown that most public-school teachers in the United States are from middle-class families. It is not surprising, then, that the schools are oriented toward middle-class norms.

The stratification system in the United States has consequences for the Negro in the area of education. From our immediately preceding discussions of income and occupational status, we should expect that the Negro would be getting less education than the white, as Negroes have a lower median income than do whites and are over-represented in low-prestige occupations. It is true that the Negro has vastly improved his educational position in this century—almost half the American Negro population was illiterate in 1900, and fifty years later the fraction was down to about one-tenth. Despite this dramatic change, Negroes have by no means achieved educational equality with whites. Among the population twenty-five years old and over, the proportion of whites who have been to college is nearly three times that of nonwhites. At the other end of the scale, only 6.6 per cent of the white population has one to four years of formal education, whereas 24.9 per cent of the nonwhites are in this category.

Under a system that forces Negroes to attend segregated schools, the quality as well as the quantity of education is lower than that for the whites. Since the ruling of the United States Supreme Court in 1954, which held racial segregation in the schools to be unconstitutional, there has been a steady—though still strongly resisted—advance in integration of the schools. This progress should mean a gradual improvement in the education of Negro pupils and ultimately should have more far-reaching effects.

Even desegregation, however, will not alone wipe out racial inequalities in opportunity. One reason is that nearly half of all American Negroes still live in the South, and in the ranking of regions according to the quality of formal education the South stands at the bottom. The southern states are, for the most part, least able to pay for schools, and they do in fact invest less per pupil than most states in other sections. This situation partly reflects rural-urban differences. The South is heavily rural, and, throughout the United States, the proportion of individuals enrolled in schools for each age category is highest in urban and lowest in rural-farm areas. Figure 7 shows both the extent of inequality of educational opportunity in the United States and the impact of Federal aid on the poor areas.

Clearly, a sizable proportion of our population is capable of absorbing more formal education than it is now given an opportunity to secure. The stratification system operates to remove some of these people from school before they have an opportunity to realize their educational potential.

Americans are fond of the local autonomy and control that have traditionally characterized the educational system in the United States. Indeed, fear of losing local control of the schools has been a powerful deterrent to acceptance of Federal aid to education. But with local financing as the price of local control, we must expect to offer—to cite contrasting examples—to children in Wilmette, Illinois, where median family income is $13,661, education of a quality vastly different from that we provide for children in Laredo, Texas, with a median family income of $2,935. We have asserted that it is shortsighted for Americans to say that population problems in Laos or Egypt or Latin America are not our concern. How much more foolhardy, then, to conclude that an underfinanced

1. Most Southern states have low per capita income.

(Average per capita income in 1964)

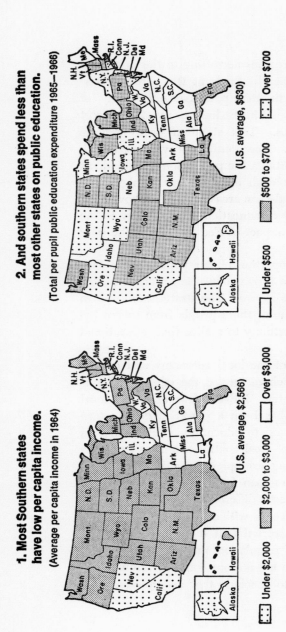

(U.S. average, $2,566)

::: Under $2,000

▓ $2,000 to $3,000

☐ Over $3,000

2. And southern states spend less than most other states on public education.

(Total per pupil public education expenditure 1965–1966)

(U.S. average, $630)

☐ Under $500

▓ $500 to $700

::: Over $700

3. This has resulted in a high rate of illiteracy in the region.

(Percentage of population 14 years old and over unable to read or write)

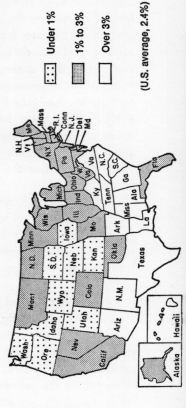

::: Under 1%

▓ 1% to 3%

☐ Over 3%

(U.S. average, 2.4%)

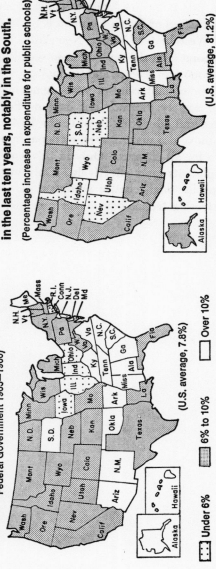

4. The Government's aid program, therefore, has concentrated on the South.
(Percentage of public education expenditure received from Federal Government 1965–1966)

(U.S. average, 7.8%)

Under 6%   6% to 10%   Over 10%

5. Because of Federal aid and increased spending by most states, total expenditures for public education have increased sharply in the last ten years, notably in the South.
(Percentage increase in expenditure for public schools)

(U.S. average, 81.2%)

Under 60%   60% to 90%   Over 90%

FIGURE 7. Educational Imbalance in the United States and Federal Efforts to Correct It
SOURCE: *The New York Times*, March 6, 1966, p. E9. © 1966 by The New York Times Company. Reprinted by permission.

school system providing inadequate education for the children of Mississippi or South Carolina is no business of the citizens of Westchester County, New York.

If we are to cope with the revolution in social organization wrought by modern science and technology, we cannot afford to confuse equalitarianism with democracy. The survival of our society depends not only on finding the brightest youths and educating them to the limits of their abilities. We must also maximize educational opportunity and motivation for all citizens. Only in this way can our society accomplish its tasks effectively. Only in this way will its citizens be intellectually equipped to enjoy the leisure that scientific technology makes possible.

CHAPTER 5

The Production and Distribution of Abundance

Urbanization and industrialization bring the development of a social and spatial organization within which both the valued and the deplored products of a complex and elaborate society are allocated. The urban mode of distribution has been built upon a folk, peasant, feudal, and industrializing past. These backgrounds influence the present state of urbanization and the system of distribution in contemporary societies throughout the world. They are the foundation upon which the process of modern urbanization develops.

The most obvious change associated with urbanization is the development of a far-reaching network of interdependent activities. This network usually proceeds from the loose linking of peasant villagers to the city through tangential interdependence with urban commercial, religious, political, or military centers to the almost complete interdependence of an urbanized world. This change in the scale of society obviously affects the ways in which the products of civilization are allocated. For example, most of the world's population lives in little communities on the fringes of urban society, where interdependence with distant urban centers is slight and limited in scope. Robert Redfield has noted the special place of "hinge people" in these communities. These representatives of limited areas of interdependence—the schoolteacher, the village priest, the merchant-traders, the representatives of distant political and military authority—have special access to the benefits of urban civilization. They act as filters or transmitters in the system of allocation centered in the city. Their power derives from limited interdependence between village and city. Their role is important today and likely to become increasingly so as interdependence increases.

Until the past couple of centuries, there has been relatively little differentiation of the labor force beyond that based on age and sex. In what we think of as the urban civilizations of the ancient world, with their soldiers, shopkeepers, philosophers, craftsmen, and statesmen, most people were farming in order to feed themselves and these few city dwellers. History is misleading in this respect: The politicians, military men, playwrights, and philosophers have left us a written record devoted largely to what they and their kind of people were doing. They make little mention of the majority of the people—the farmers, miners, and other laborers. Most people in ancient Greece

were peasants, not sculptors; we sing of knights and trou-
badours, but most people in medieval Europe were serfs.
Only within the last 200 years, with the technological
applications of scientific discoveries, have societies existed
in which large proportions of the populations learned occupational roles differentiated from one another on grounds
other than age and sex status.

Throughout the greatest part of human history, most
workers secured their own raw materials and owned their
own tools. They worked under their own roofs on their
own time and gauged their market—that is, they determined both the quality and quantity of what they produced
and sold the finished product to consumers.

Being human, we tend to think that our time and our
society are the normal ones and that all other ones are
exotic and strange. But from a historical and sociological
perspective, our society is unique. People lived in one
way economically and socially until the past century and
a half or so. We are the ones who are trying an experiment in economic and social life. Indeed, when we discuss
preindustrial systems of production, it doesn't make much
difference what geographic location or historical period
we pick as an example because the organization of economic life was essentially the same 300 years ago and
10,000 years ago. The big shift has come in the last couple
of centuries.

The Industrial Revolution: A Sociological Perspective

Almost any one of our ancestors 10,000 years ago was
either hunting or fishing for a living or engaging in agriculture at a fairly primitive level. The basic pattern of his

economic and social life was the same, no matter where he lived 5,000 or 10,000 years ago. A hunter made his own spear or bow and arrow: He found his own raw materials. He did his own hunting, which is to say he turned out his own finished product. He made his own decisions about whether he should spend his time looking for a couple of rabbits a day or one caribou a week. In other words, he regulated the quality and quantity of his production. He also "marketed" his own finished product, which consisted of dragging it home for himself and his family. The whole economic process was wrapped up in the individual. He obtained his raw materials, he used them to fashion a finished product, and he consumed it.

If, from that point 10,000 years ago, we jump forward about 9,700 years, we find things changed very little. Our ancestors living in Europe in 1650 or 1700 still functioned with an economic process centered in the individual. Most of them were farmers. But even those who at that time played rather complex economic roles as craftsmen—perhaps 2 per cent of the population 300 years ago—were living essentially the same economic life that the hunter had lived. Such a craftsman—a dagger maker in Toledo, Spain, for example—secured his own raw materials, bought his ore at the dock, smelted it, worked it in a forge with his own tools under his own roof; indeed, he probably lived in the building where he worked. He gauged his own market, deciding whether he was better off attempting to sell a hundred flimsy daggers every month or only one dagger of highest quality; whether it was better to establish a reputation as a man who made the best daggers for a good price but sold only a few or as a man from whom you could get a dagger tomorrow if you broke yours today (and you were likely to break it because of the quality of the merchandise he turned out). He thus determined quality and quantity. When he was through making his daggers, he sold them. Some people came to his shop to pick up their daggers. Occasionally he went around the countryside to trade fairs, set up a stand, and marketed his product. With the money he made he returned to the seaside to buy more iron ore, took it back home, smelted it, made more daggers, and sold them. But all of this changed.

A couple of centuries ago several factors made it possible to implement an enormously important social invention. (Ideas are invented just as machines are.) The social invention was mass production. What happened to the cloth industry in England is a good example. Previously, linen makers had grown flax in their own backyards, had harvested it themselves, and in their own homes had converted the flax into linen thread, the linen thread into cloth, and the cloth into a product. They had taken it to the town, sold it, supported their families with the proceeds, and planted more flax. The economic process was still wrapped up in the individual.

The social structure began to change when an entrepreneur, an individual capitalist, took over some of these operations. What such a man did was to acquire a good deal of raw materials, more than he himself could work on. Instead of growing flax outside his house and owning his own spinning wheel and loom, for example, he purchased more flax than he could possibly process by himself. He then made agreements with a number of cottagers around the countryside, deposited a certain amount of the flax with each of them, picked up linen they had finished, took it to town, and sold it. And he came back the next week, having taken the proceeds, the money from selling his linen, and bought more flax; he passed this new flax out to his cottagers and picked up what linen they had finished that week, took it to town, and sold it. In other words, the entrepreneur greatly altered what had been the universal system of human work throughout history. Now it was the entrepreneur, not the worker, who secured the raw materials and gauged the market. It was he who brought the flax, took the linen, paid off the workers, and sold the finished product.

Notice what has happened. The worker himself no longer gets his own raw materials, and he no longer markets his own finished product. He is still using his own tools, rather like the hunter of an earlier age. He is still working under his own roof, like the dagger maker. He is still working on his own time and determining the quality and quantity of his own product. But he's not selling it to the consumer, and he's not getting his own raw materials. These two ends of the economic process have been taken away from the worker.

Once this first step was taken, the Industrial Revolution came fast. (Social revolutions are really much more interesting than political ones. Fewer people are killed outright, but change occurs swiftly and affects many people.) A man bright enough to be an entrepreneur soon saw that he was spending a great amount of time driving around the countryside in his wagon when he could have been in town operating in the market. So he moved into town. The entrepreneur bought spinning wheels, put them in a building, and hired cottagers to come into town.

Here are the essentials of mass production. There is a factory, with all workers in one location. A capitalist owns the tools they work with, the roof they work under, and the raw materials. He takes the product and sells it. A labor force in the modern sense of the term has been created.

The entrepreneur discovers that he can hire one man, not to spin or to weave, but simply to watch and see that everybody else works. That man (who will more than pay for his wages in increased productivity) we call the "foreman." He earns his wages by seeing that the other people work; he supervises the production process. At this point, the whole relationship between the worker and the economic process has been changed. The worker doesn't get his own raw materials. He doesn't work with his own tools under his own roof. He doesn't sell the product. And he doesn't determine the time when he'll work on it. This set of social changes is what Karl Marx called "the separation of the workers from the means of production."

With men working under supervision, a foreman might soon notice that one man can spin very well. He's very good at spinning thread, say, but inefficient on the loom. He doesn't weave too well. A couple of chairs away from him is a man who weaves cloth rapidly and well but is slow and inefficient as a spinner. There is an obvious solution to this problem. The first man is put to spinning thread full time. Then the thread is passed to the next man who weaves cloth full time. Here is the essence of mass production. All that remains is the manufacture of replaceable parts. With replaceable parts for the machinery and with occupational specialists on the line passing partly finished products to other men to finish, the Industrial Revolution is complete.

As a result of this economic revolution, several important

alterations occurred in the social structure. For efficiency, people were aggregated; this step was the beginning of modern urbanism. Then, with fixed capital, the entrepreneur had money tied up in one place, which cut down his mobility in a way that the domestic system did not. Formerly, if it was not a good year for linen, the entrepreneur who had been running around the countryside picking up his linen and leaving his flax with cottagers had only to take what capital he had accumulated and go into something else. But, as soon as he bought the building in town and filled it with spinning wheels, the entrepreneur tied himself to a great deal of capital that could not be moved: fixed capital. The entrepreneur of the eighteenth century may not have had a great deal of fixed capital by the standards of General Motors, but he had a great deal for those days.

With the factory system and fixed capital came another crucial change in the social structure: free labor. Back in the guildsman's day, serfs belonged to a manor; they had rights in the land. The serfs had to give a certain portion of their labor or produce to the baron because they were allowed to live on the land and received protection from him. This kind of social order was foreign to a mass-production, fixed-capital economy. In a mass-production economy, people must be able, when business gets bad, to move somewhere else. This free labor is an essential part of the modern economic system, because the entrepreneur has his money tied up in fixed capital and the easiest cost to reduce is labor cost. He lays off people until he needs more productivity, and then he hires them again.

Factory production, fixed capital, and free labor—all

are characteristics of the Industrial Revolution; all have consequences in an industrial social order. Against this background, let us examine some of the economic trends in our own industrial society.

The Dominance of the Corporation

The American Telephone and Telegraph Company's gross revenues in 1965 were more than twice as large as those of the largest state in the United States, as shown in Figure 8. This simple measure of sheer size suggests the central importance that the corporate form of organization plays in industrial economies. The corporation is not confined to capitalistic economies; it is found also under socialism. For example, the nationalization of banking and coal mining in Britain modified only slightly the essential corporate forms of organization and control of those enterprises. The Soviet Union has developed most of her state-controlled and state-managed industrial organizations along corporate lines.

A corporation is recognized in American law as a legal personality with many of the rights and duties of an individual, and it may enter into contracts, but the controls that may be exercised over it are not exactly those that society may exercise over an individual. Corporations are the property of many individuals, yet particular men run them. They make decisions on policy and practice, thus affecting the lives of workers and consumers. Corporate organization influences our productive capacity, our financial system, the employment of labor, and the buying habits of citizens.

In the United States, 95 per cent of business firms have

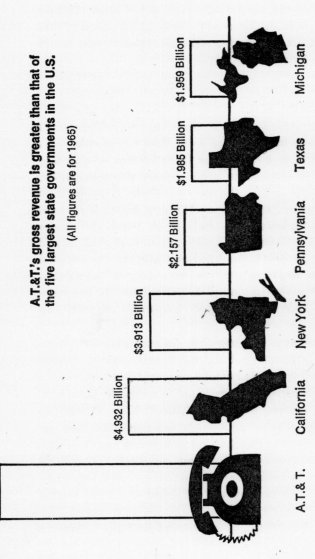

A.T.&T.'s gross revenue is greater than that of the five largest state governments in the U.S.

(All figures are for 1965)

$11.062 Billion $4.932 Billion $3.913 Billion $2.157 Billion $1.985 Billion $1.959 Billion

A.T.&T.   California   New York   Pennsylvania   Texas   Michigan

FIGURE 8. Comparison of 1965 Gross Revenue of American Telephone and Telegraph Company with That of Five Largest State Governments in the United States

SOURCE: *The New York Times,* June 12, 1966, p. E4. © 1966 by The New York Times Company. Reprinted by permission.

fewer than twenty employees. A glance at these statistics might lead us to the conclusion that small businesses dominate the economy, but that is not the case. The firms with fewer than twenty employees account for fewer than one-fourth of the wage-earners and salaried workers in the economy. The other three-fourths are employed by the corporate giants, which comprise only 5 per cent of the total number of firms. More than one-third of all American workers are in firms that have 1,000 or more employees.

The extent of corporate concentration varies greatly among industries. It is greatest in manufacturing, transportation, and public utilities. In utilities, for example, more than two-thirds of the employees work for firms of 1,000 employees or more. On the other hand, in construction, service industries, and retail trade, from 40 to 50 per cent of the workers are in firms employing fewer than twenty people.

Even if we define as "small" those companies with assets of up to $1 million, the small companies have less than 13 per cent of the market. Furthermore, they operate on smaller profit margins than do large companies. Companies with fewer than 500 employees (and they include more than 99 per cent of all private business firms) receive less than 20 per cent of the military contracts. Furthermore, in both share of total sales and share of total profits, the long-run trend is against the small business.

The Composition of the American Labor Force

The labor force of this country has grown steadily, in keeping with our rising population. In 1890 it consisted of 22.2 million people, or about 23 per cent of the total population. In 1940 it was 53 million, or 40 per cent of the people. In 1950 it was more than 63 million, and by 1960 it had exceeded 70 million. The proportion of the total population represented in the labor force for the past few decades has remained slightly higher than 40 per cent. This leveling off of the fraction of the total population in the labor force can be explained by the disappearance of child labor, the increase in automation, and the changing age distribution of the population.

A second important feature of our labor force is the increasing number of women gainfully employed. Even more striking has been the increase in the number of married and divorced women in the labor force. Although half a century ago only a negligible proportion of the labor force was composed of married women, now nearly a third of the workers in the labor force are women, most of them married and living with their husbands. The increase in the number of gainfully employed women, both married and single, is of course only one aspect of the changing status of women in our society.

The revolution in educational expectations has had its impact on the labor force too. Whereas half the young men from fourteen to nineteen years old were in the labor force in 1890, only a third of the men in this age group are job-seekers or job-holders today.

Also, the proportion of men who continue to participate in the labor force after they are sixty-five has declined from more than two-thirds in 1890 to about 30 per cent in 1960. This change is attributable largely to the increase in pension programs and in the practice of making retirement compulsory at a given age.

The total amount of time expended in work in our society is less than one might think. Not only do many of the added millions of workers in the labor force (especially the women) limit themselves to part-time employment, but also the length of the work week itself has been greatly reduced. The standard work week in 1900 was fifty-four to sixty hours or more; a person steadily employed in a manufacturing plant thus worked about 3,000 hours a year. Today such a worker averages fewer than forty hours a week and receives a paid vacation, putting in only about 2,000 hours a year.

Not only the composition of the labor force, but also its distribution among various occupational statuses, has changed markedly in the past few generations. At the time our country was founded, farming was the most important income-producing activity of the people. And as recently as 1870, more than half the labor force was engaged in agriculture. Today farmers comprise only 6 per cent of the labor force.

The major industrial change in the last century has been from the production of goods to the production of services. At the turn of the century, about three-fourths of the people in the labor force were engaged in producing physical goods, and fewer than one-fourth provided services. By 1960 the majority of the people in the labor force worked in service occupations. These figures include employers and the self-employed, as well as wage-earners and salaried workers. This large-scale shift in the distribution of the labor force has been brought about largely by technological improvements. Machines wash dishes, dig ditches, and even measure and make corrections in the quality of production by other machines. Heavy manual labor has given way to machine production, which has freed a larger portion of the labor force for work in service industries. It is not simply that automation has taken over many of the tasks formerly performed by human hands in manufacturing; agriculture too has become more and more mechanized. There were 600,000 fewer farms in the United States in 1954 than in 1950.

Despite the fact that there are now fewer farms than at any time since 1890, these farms are able, through mechanization, to supply a considerably greater population than could a larger number of smaller farms. In 1900, 37.5 per cent of all Americans at work were doing farm jobs. Today, only 6 per cent of our labor force works on farms—and these workers are able to produce surpluses. The trend toward mechanization of agriculture and manufacturing has meant that a larger and larger segment of the labor force is available to run laundromats, rent out evening clothes, provide package-delivery services, be tree surgeons or public stenographers—in short, to enter service industries.

This change in the industrial structure from production to service is accompanied, of course, by a change in the occupational distribution of the labor force. The most dramatic growth has occurred in semiskilled labor and the clerical occupations; the most striking decline is in the unskilled segment of the labor force. The increase in clerical and professional personnel is a corollary of the expansion of services; most of the people in both these categories are providing services. Since 1890, clerical workers in the labor force have increased fivefold, professional and technical workers threefold, sales workers nearly twofold, and proprietors and managers by almost one-half. During the same period, household workers declined 50 per cent, but other service workers, like barbers, beauticians, cooks, firemen, janitors, policemen, and wait-resses, have doubled. In general, the proportions in serv-ice occupations have increased by a third.

The nation's economy, then, is less and less dependent on muscle power and more and more dependent on pro-fessional, technical, and clerical skills. The shift from brawn and manpower to education and brainpower sum-marizes a basic trend in American economic life.

The growth of semiskilled labor at the expense of the unskilled is a function of two changes in the industrial structure. First, of course, was the development of ma-chinery that enables one semiskilled worker to perform the task formerly accomplished by several unskilled laborers. One crane operator, for example, can replace twenty men pushing wheelbarrows. The other change that has helped to speed the mechanization of industry was the success of the labor-union movement during the past three decades, which has made labor more expensive and thus has made it more profitable, for example, to hire one man and pur-chase a machine than to use three men and save the cost of the machine.

The average weekly earnings of production workers rose from $23.25 in 1930 to $92.00 in 1960. To some extent, of course, this improvement in laborers' wages weakens the labor-union movement. Any organization dedicated to conflict or social change, whether the N.A.A.C.P or suf-fragettes, loses some of its momentum as the practices it opposes are revised and it achieves its goals. In 1960 there were 17 million union members in a total work force of more than 73 million. Between 1953 and 1960, while the total labor force increased from 67,362,000 to 73,126,000, the number of workers in unions decreased more than 2 per cent. At the end of 1961, George Meany reported that AFL–CIO membership had decreased by nearly 200,-000 in two years. Of the 17 million workers organized into unions, only a few more than 2 million are white-collar workers.

Work and Purpose

People work in order to obtain the goods and services they want. Hunters stalk game so that they may convert the meat into food, the hides into clothing and dwellings, the bones into weapons for more hunting. In an industrial society, people work to earn money, which they can use to satisfy their needs and wants for economic goods and services.

But people are motivated to work for other reasons as well. If they were not, why would the man who earns $50,000 a year put in extra hours striving for a promotion and a raise, or why would the man who inherited enough wealth to live comfortably do the work necessary to get through professional school and then show up at an office every day? Why do sociologists who study industrial organization find it not unusual for a member of a small work group in a factory to turn down a chance for promotion to a job as foreman, accompanied by a raise in pay?

Both the wealthy man who continues to work and the worker who rejects a promotion illustrate the fact that there are incentives governing work that are not economic. People are motivated to pursue economic activity not only to make money but also to gain power and prestige, to cultivate and maintain primary-group relations, to contribute to a sense of purpose, and to fulfill the expectations of other social roles, especially those of husband and father. The worker who would rather stay with his production gang than be promoted is willing, perhaps, to forgo economic gain for the feeling of "belonging" that he enjoys as a member of the primary group.

Many people who have enough wealth to permit them to enjoy full-time leisure choose to work. Noteworthy contemporary examples, of course, are the Rockefellers and the Kennedys. (Wisecracks about politics aside, top-level government service is grueling work.) Part of the training one receives to be a member of American society is learning that work is expected of him. It is one of the basic norms of American culture that healthy adult males ought to be engaged in something productive. It is not uncommon for people who have retired to complain of feeling useless; they have lost the sense of purpose that their work gave them.

Changes in Personal Income and Spending Patterns

Certainly the Industrial Revolution has brought drastic changes in production and consumption patterns. With 7 per cent of the world's land area and only 6 per cent of its population, the United States produces more than one-third of the world's goods. The average work week in the United States has been reduced by about one-third in this century, whereas production per man hour has tripled. During the past sixty years, family income has increased two and a half times in purchasing power. During the same period, the proportion of Americans who own their own homes has increased from one in three to three in five.

Total personal income in the United States from all sources has risen steadily since 1950. The aggregate personal income of $228.5 billion in 1950 more than doubled to $530.7 billion by 1965. More important, there has been a continuous rise in the amount available to spend. Personal disposable income of Americans more than doubled from $207.7 billion in 1950 to $465.3 billion in 1965.

American society has experienced recently a remarkable redistribution of income. As the amount of education and the number of white-collar workers have increased, the pyramid of income has been altered. It is no longer a perfect pyramid; indeed, it is becoming more and more diamond-shaped: Instead of a few people who are very rich and many who are very poor, there are few at either pole. Most Americans fall near the middle of the income distribution.

In 1929, 87 per cent of American families had incomes of less than $5,000 a year. Look what has happened during the ensuing thirty years. As recently as 1936, a diagram

TABLE 1

Percentage of Multiple-Person Families Receiving Given Incomes, Before Taxes, at Selected Dates

Income Bracket	Date			
	1935–1936	*1947*	*1953*	*1960*
Less than $4,000	68%	37%	28%	23%
$4,000 to $5,999	17	29	28	23
$6,000 to $7,499	6	12	17	16
$7,500 to $14,999	7	17	23	31
$15,000 or more	2	4	5	7

(All income distribution figures are expressed in 1960 dollars.)

SOURCE: Adapted from data presented in "Poverty and Deprivation in the United States," pamphlet issued by the Conference on Economic Progress, Washington, D.C., 1963.

of the distribution of income among American families would have been a pyramid. But during the 1940s, with the enormous demand for labor, service workers and man-

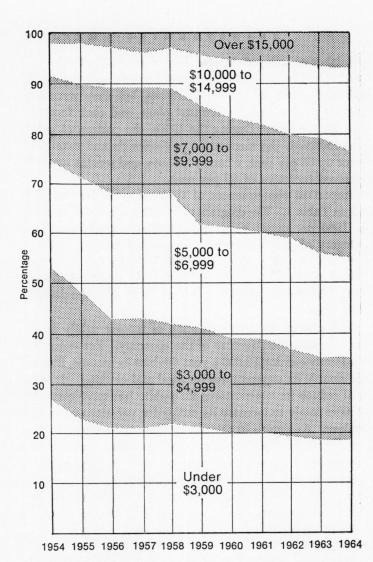

FIGURE 9. Percentage of United States Families by
Total Money Income, 1954–1964

SOURCE: U.S. Department of Commerce, Bureau of the Census, *Current Population Reports*, Series P-60, No. 47, Table C.

ual laborers enjoyed income increases of about 180 per cent. In the same decade, professionals and managers achieved relatively smaller increases, but they were the highest paid workers in the first place, and their incomes rose 96 per cent. During the 1950s, the pattern of gains was reversed: the incomes of professionals and managers went up 68 per cent, whereas laborers and service workers received increases of 39 per cent.

Important consequences of these changes are brought out in Table 1. The diagram of family income distribution in 1960 no longer even approximates a pyramid. The category of people receiving incomes of less than $4,000 —the vast majority of our population twenty-five years ago —had been reduced by two-thirds. As Figure 9 shows, this redistribution trend has continued through the decade 1954–1964.

This change in the distribution of income subtly feeds back to alter the structure of the economy. For example, if a family earning $3,000 a year doubles its income, it does not double its expenditures for food and clothing. It may well reduce its expenditures for public transportation. It is more likely to increase its outlay for vacations or stock-brokers. As Figure 10 shows, the average American urban family, while experiencing a rise in income, reduces its proportional expenditures for food and clothing and increases its outlay for housing, automobiles, and medical care. The redistribution of income in a society experiencing a science-based revolution in its industrial complex is a basic cause of the growth of the service sector of the economy.

Similarly, scientific technology and mass production bring changes to patterns of consumer behavior. At an

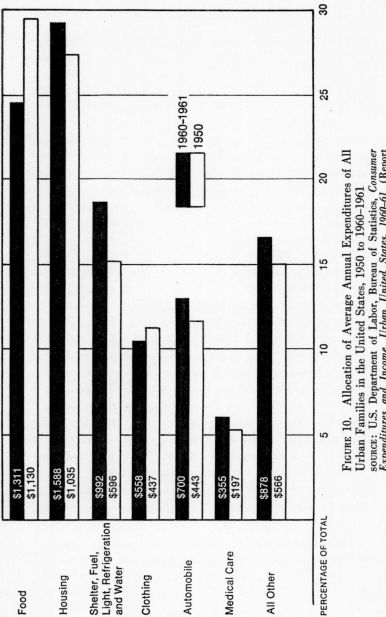

FIGURE 10. Allocation of Average Annual Expenditures of All
Urban Families in the United States, 1950 to 1960–1961
SOURCE: U.S. Department of Labor, Bureau of Statistics, *Consumer
Expenditures and Income, Urban United States, 1960–61* (Report
No. 237–8, April 1964).

earlier date, say 1890, the ordinary buyer in a small town or rural trading center purchased goods that were usually of a quality not very difficult to determine. On the basis of what he could see, touch, or taste, he could decide whether or not to buy. Today in modern retailing—rural or urban—the customer is in a different position.

The quality, durability, and utility of goods are not well standardized in relation to price. The research of consumers' testing agencies suggests that the less expensive of two competing products is frequently the one of higher quality. The more expensive product may capture a sizable share of the market, however, by skillful advertising and packaging.

The nature of retailing has changed greatly. The department store, the mail-order house, the chain store, and the discount store all give witness to the growing complexity of the market, to alterations in the earlier competitive patterns, and to changes in the role of the ultimate consumer. Chain and discount stores are a good reflection of business enterprise in mass society. They are efficient —they eliminate the middleman and handle standardized goods—but their merchandising tends to be impersonal.

The changes in income distribution wrought by a mass-production economy are startling; the shift from the traditional pyramidal social structure to a society characterized by a huge middle class is impressive. But more impressive than the shift in income distribution is its consequence: a change in style of life. Frederick Lewis Allen, the social historian, tells us:

For instance, consider the matter of personal appearance, remembering that in 1900 the frock-coated, silk-hatted banker and his Paris-gowned wife were recognizable at a distance, if they ventured among the common herd, as beings apart. Forty or fifty years ago the countryman in a metropolis was visibly a "hayseed"; the purchaser of inexpensive men's clothing was betrayed by his tight-waisted jackets and bulbous-toed shoes. Today the difference in appearance between a steelworker (or a clerk) and a high executive is hardly noticeable to the casual eye. . . . And there is many a man with an income in six figures (before taxes) and with thousands of employees who, though his suit may be a little better cut than those of most of the men about him on a New York subway train or a transcontinental plane, attracts no curious notice at all; he looks just about like everybody else.

As for women, the difference in appearance between the one who spends $5,000 a year on clothes and the one who spends only a small fraction of that is by no means as conspicuous as the difference between the woman who has good taste and the woman who lacks it. The fact that the wealthy woman has thirty dresses to the poor woman's three is not visible on the street, and the fact that her dresses are made of better materials and are better cut is observable only by the expert eye at close range. . . .

Consider for a moment a contrast with regard to those [nylon] stockings. At the turn of the century silk stockings were a mark of luxury. In the year 1900, in a nation of 75 million people, only 155,000 pairs were manufactured. In the year 1949 the American sales of nylon stockings—considered by most people at least as fine as silk, if not finer—were not 155,000 but 543 *million* pairs: enough to provide every female in the country, from the age of fourteen up, with between nine and ten pairs apiece.*

As Allen goes on to point out, clothing is only one example of the breakdown of economic barriers between styles of living. Differences are minimal in the quality of many everyday items used by rich man and poor man:

* Frederick Lewis Allen, *The Big Change* (New York: Harper & Brothers [now Harper & Row], 1952), pp. 219–20.

cigarettes, razors, radios, automobiles, home lighting, plumbing. This fact does not mean a trend toward uniformity and conformity but rather a diversity of choice, based to a great extent upon region or personal preference rather than upon social class.

Finally, our economy has changed because alterations have been made in the use of credit. Many consumers no longer pay cash or use open charge accounts. Rather, they pay on some sort of fixed installment plan. Installment buying has become a culture pattern for large sections of our population, and the charges for this service are passed on, in one form or another, to the consumer.

Individual indebtedness, once viewed in the United States on a scale ranging from unfortunate to immoral, is now an accepted practice. Indeed, individual indebtedness has increased drastically since World War II, at the same time that, contrary to popular myth, Federal indebtedness on a per capita basis has actually declined. The Federal debt was $1,911.14 per capita in 1946, $1,574.80 in 1961. Over the same period, average private indebtedness soared from $424 to $1,687.

Industrialization has brought great aggregate wealth and made possible social and cultural advantages for most people, but many of our social problems can be attributed to the uneven impact of our economic progress.

Human welfare cannot be measured exclusively in terms of aggregate economic position. The high level of industrialization that we have attained and that has been the basis of our great wealth also has given rise to new economic and social problems.

Per capita personal disposable income in the United States is rapidly approaching $2,500 a year, which means that theoretically every man, woman, and child in the

United States would have that much to spend. But our income distribution is such that many *families* do not have even that much. From 1947 to 1964 the percentage of families with annual incomes of less than $3,000 declined from 31 in 1947 to 18 in 1964. The number of families with annual incomes of $10,000 and over more than tripled, from 7 per cent in 1947 to 22 per cent in 1964.

The movement of our population from farm to city and from city to suburb, the problems of urban transportation, the pollution of the air we breathe and the water we drink, unemployment resulting from automation and the changing demands of industry—all these and many other problems are attributable in large part to our industrial development and affect the quality of our lives.

A Crucial Question for Americans

How can we keep our enormously complex economy in the role of our servant, without allowing its requirements to structure our national purpose and inhibit our opportunities for individual self-realization?

Automation, by its very virtue in accelerating production, has pushed us still further into the position in which a constant consumer demand is essential to our economic health. Even in agriculture, we must take drastic steps to avoid a fluctuating market. At present, the Federal Government has $4.5 billion worth of surplus farm produce in storage. Simply the cost of storing it comes to about $1 billion a year. How did we get into a situation in which fixed demand is so crucial a matter? We stabilized the cost of labor at the same time that we were increasing the amount of fixed capital.

Most of our engineering technology in the last century and a half has been put to inventing and perfecting machines that make products—production machines. It is only recently that we have developed machines that perform such formerly expensive and time-consuming tasks as quality testing and readjustment of the production-line machines. When whole factories are automated, fixed capital will take on new meaning.

By the standards of an automated economy, our present fixed capital is inadequate. The Industrial Revolution is only beginning. The concept of fixed capital brings to mind huge factories with big steel machines that cannot be picked up and moved. Think of the meaning of fixed capital when one machine is running another machine, so that the greatest expense is not in turning out the product but in stopping the machine. At this point, fixed capital reaches the point at which the costliest thing one can do is to cease production. A stable market, a steady demand, become essential.

These changes have been accompanied by corporate concentration, by the separation of ownership from control in American industry. Most of the functions that used to be performed by entrepreneurs—owner-proprietors—are now performed by salaried managers. The large individual business is owned, not by one man who can run it, but, as some institutional advertising tells us, by millions of people. The stockholders among whom this diversified ownership is spread do own their companies. But they delegate control of the corporation to salaried management. The *owners* of the corporation do not dominate it as individuals. In some respects, the differences in the occupational roles of the managers of a Russian factory and of an American factory are not so extreme as they seem at first glance. Modern industrial systems, no matter what their economic norms and political goals, are staffed and run by salaried managers.

Of crucial importance for understanding the politics of industrial society is a trend that sociologists (following Maine, a nineteenth-century historian) describe as movement from status to contract. In medieval times the serfs had the land because of their status, because of who they were. A baron was a baron for the same reason: His grandfather had been a baron, and the position was his right. The serfs owed him certain obligations, not because of some peculiar occupational training they had had, not because of achievement, but because each man was born into his status.

By the time the cottagers were moved into town to work in factories, this structure was crumbling. No longer did people owe these kinds of obligations simply because of the positions they occupied. The closest approximation to the old feudal system in an industrial situation is the small one-company town that survives for generations. Suppose a worker in this kind of situation falls ill. There is no unemployment compensation. But none is needed, because a system of mutual obligations exists. When a man is ill, the owner's wife comes by with a basket of groceries and asks if there is anything she can do to help, and people who work with him will offer to help him and his family. This situation is a status system, a system of mutual obligations. In a larger economy, in which most people work for big organizations, contracts are substituted for this kind of status system. We do not expect Mrs. Henry Ford to appear with baskets of groceries at the homes of unskilled laborers who are sick. Instead, the government arranges a contract substitute.

Wherever there is a social need that the baron would have met for the serfs or the serfs would have filled for one another, the trend is toward having the government contract an obligation. Taxpayers contract with the national government for defense and with the local government for education. Nineteenth-century Americans nursed their aged relatives at home; twentieth-century Americans pay taxes for Medicare.

We are no longer a society of rural villages and independent entrepreneurs. The economic and political institutions of an urban-industrial society are inextricably interwoven because, in the shift from status to contract as a principle of social organization, wage contracts alone replace only a small part of the total system of mutual obligations. The history of our learning to live with urbanization and industrialization is a history of the process of negotiating supplementary contracts. We start with a wage contract, but we supplement it with a social-security contract, an unemployment-insurance contract, Medicare, and so on. It is this system that industrial societies—democratic or totalitarian, capitalist or socialist—have devised as a substitute for the mutual-obligation system found where institutions tend to be coterminous, where familial, economic, and political functions derive from the same group.

The question is not whether or not such supplementary contracts will exist in an industrial social order but how to maintain maximum individual freedom in such a context.

CHAPTER 6

The Politics
of Industrialization
and the Industrialization
of Politics

Former F.B.I. agent Jack Levine claims that, of the 8,500 members of the Communist Party in the United States, nearly 1,500 are F.B.I. informants. With one-sixth of the dues-paying members, the F.B.I. is undoubtedly the largest single financial contributor to the American Communist Party. Obviously, the maintenance of internal order in a modern society is a complex study. Nor is the maintenance of external order, the protection of the society from outside threats, a secondary matter in an age of thermonuclear weapons and space satellites. A task that, among our ancestors, was a part-time duty for a tribal chief and his war council is an enormous industry in the United States.

The application of science and technology to the economic process has made possible mass production of goods. Mass production is profitable because modern transportation makes mass distribution possible and modern techniques of communication help to create and sustain a mass market. This combination of mass production and mass consumption pushes out the boundaries of a society. Hundreds of millions of people can now participate in a single social system. They can keep in touch with one another. They can share wants, and they can share means for satisfying those wants. A person can sit in Los Angeles and watch a television program originating in New York. Another person can watch the same program at the same time in London, where it is received via Telstar. Relatives of either viewer may be serving their governments in Asia, Africa, Latin America—or outer space. When social systems achieve such size and complexity, their governments become enormous establishments. As industrialization revolutionizes economies, it necessarily exerts an impact on governments. As industries grow into far-flung corporate enterprises, so do the governments supervising their activities expand into many-armed bureaucracies.

In the United States government, in the executive branch alone, there are approximately 2,000 agencies, bureaus, and departments and more than 5,000 advisory bureaus. There are 2.5 million men in the armed forces and nearly an equal number of Federal civil servants. A measure of the extent of the industrialization of politics is William J. Lederer's estimate that there are twice as many government public-relations men in Washington as there are journalists.

Some notion of the size of government and its role in the market can be gained by examining government as a consumer in an economy of mass consumption. Of our present Gross National Product, about 70 per cent is purchased by individual consumers and 10 per cent by business. Federal, state, and local governments spend enough to consume the other 20 per cent of the country's total GNP each year.

One consequence of the impact of the scientific revolution on government is the reciprocal impact of government on science. According to John H. Rubel, Assistant Secretary of Defense and Deputy Director of Research and Engineering in the Department of Defense, three-fourths of all research and development funds in the United States are supplied by the Federal Government. He estimates that about one-half of all the scientists and engineers engaged in research and development in this country are being supported by Defense Department funds.

The Expansion of Government Power

One of the most striking changes in modern life is the expansion of the government into areas of action long considered outside the direct scope of the state. This expansion is particularly visible in economic institutions, but it is evident in almost all other important segments of the society. The manner in which the state tends to become an all-embracing, controlling agency depends to a great extent upon the cultural values and practices of a particular time and place. In most democratic countries the major

trend has been in the direction of administrative regulation of capitalistic enterprises and of furnishing certain
public services. On the whole, such trends have not yet
greatly disturbed the familial, religious, and economic institutions of democratic societies. In authoritarian countries the state has taken over property and economic
enterprise almost entirely, with more and more regimenta-
tion and planning of nearly every aspect of public and
private life.

The forms of control, however, are in the long run perhaps secondary to their meanings for individuals and
groups within the large society. It is quite conceivable
that under our representative system the idea may emerge
that government is in essence administrative. If this view
becomes accepted in practice, the United States could con-
ceivably move toward a totalitarian pattern. On the other
hand, if the essential division of governmental functions
into legislative, executive, and judicial remains, such a
complete identification of government with administration
may be prevented.

There are various ways to measure the expansion of
functions in the political order. The most apparent indi-
cators are increases in the cost of government and in
numbers of public personnel. Others are the growth in
services and regulation. The extension of the political
structure is easily seen in the increasing proportion of the
labor force employed by the government. The percentage
of the labor force employed by the government has increased in the past century nearly five times as fast as has
the number of privately employed workers. In 1850, 7.2
million Americans were privately employed; only about
200,000 were government employees. By 1960, the figure

for the privately employed had risen to nearly 60 million, but the number of government employees had skyrocketed to 10.5 million.

A further indication of the trend toward government's taking responsibility for many aspects of social life is revealed in patterns of taxation. A quarter of a century ago, 14 per cent of the national income went for taxes. Today 31 per cent of the national income goes to taxes. (These figures include all taxes: Federal, state, and local.) The centralization of government is shown by the growing proportion of taxes collected by the Federal government: At the turn of the century it received less than one-fifth of all taxes collected in the United States; that fraction has grown to three-fourths.

It is true that our society is much larger in population and in geographic area than it used to be, but the major share of governmental expansion in personnel and budget is attributable to increases in services provided by the government. The state now assumes at least some of the responsibility for caring for the aged, the mentally ill, and the unemployed, as well as for providing the entire citizenry with postal service, highways, schools, parks, and many other services. It also regulates, in varying degrees, the currency, the mass media of communication, interstate transportation, the quality of foods and drugs, and numerous other enterprises regarded as needing supervision in the public interest.

The single largest expenditure of government in the United States is for the preservation of external order through the diplomatic and military structures. In addition to financing our own military forces, we spend billions of dollars annually helping to support the military forces and economies of other societies. The economic aid that we furnish to other countries accounts for considerably less than half our foreign expenditures, the bulk of which go to military aid. Furthermore, the trend in the past decade has been to broaden the geographic distribution of our foreign expenditures. One result of these efforts toward the maintenance of external order is that the political structure is intertwined with the political and economic institutions of a large share of the other nations in the world.

Political and Economic Interdependence

That modern nations can scarcely be economically self-sufficient is apparent. Interdependence has been greatly increased by the rise and spread of industry, which requires raw materials from widely scattered sources. In fact, in the century preceding World War I, an economic world order of a kind had arisen despite the persistence in some nations of tariffs and other limitations on free trade. The restrictive nature of much of the world's trade today is related to shifts in the balance of political power that have been under way for some time; nonetheless, economic interdependence is clear. We purchase and use foodstuffs, clothes, implements, tools, machines, and recreational goods that are made of raw materials from all over the world. Our breakfast coffee, tea, or cocoa comes from afar, as do the tin and bauxite that go into kitchen utensils used in preparing the meal. People ride to work in motor vehicles that could not be made without imported tin, bauxite, chromium, and rubber. The automobile requires materials from eighteen different countries; beauty shops use products from seventeen and clothing manufacturers from twenty-one. The electrical-goods industry imports from seventeen countries and the jewelers from twenty-one. Radio manufacturing is dependent on eighteen items from abroad, the stationery-supplies industry on twenty-four, and the telephone network on fifteen.

The United States, in turn, exports great quantities of coal, copper, gypsum, lead, petroleum, phosphate rock, silver, and zinc. Meats, dairy products, apples, tobacco, wheat, and lumber are shipped abroad in large amounts. Of manufactured articles the most important exports are automobiles, electrical machinery, engines, hardware, farm equipment, sewing machines, firearms, cotton goods, motion pictures, and rubber products.

In order to move goods and services from region to region and from country to country, the world has been covered with a network of land, sea, and air transport and communication lines. From the turn of the present century to the outbreak of World War II, the marine tonnage in the world increased 136 per cent. To facilitate transportation, common navigation rules have been worked out through international agreements. Similarly, uniform freight rates on shipping lines operating in the same regions or between the same ports have been generally agreed upon. Long before the coming of the railroad, many of the larger rivers of the world were "internationalized" for traffic, and all sorts of provisions for the use of port facilities were made. In Europe particularly, international arrangements were developed to facilitate railway transport across the thousands of miles of political boundaries. Uniform bills of lading, reciprocal use of rolling stock, agreements fixing responsibility for damages, coordinated timetables, and many other common practices were adopted. There were also agreements among European nations to aid in motor-transport services.

The development of air transport is even more striking. In the two decades separating the two world wars, airplane lines reached into every part of the globe. Almost overnight the most remote regions came within relatively easy flying distance. In 1947 a treaty established the International Civil Aviation Organization, with twenty-six nations participating. This institution set up basic standards for global air traffic.

The international postal service, the Universal Postal Union, was established in 1874 and, except during wartime, embraces practically the entire habitable globe in a single world-wide postal area. The development of radio communication followed a somewhat similar course. Following earlier monopolistic patterns, international agreements were made regarding commercial radio and the use of radio in shipping. Since World War I, radio broadcasting has become not only commercially but also politically one of the most important media of communication to the masses.

The telephone and, later, radio-telephony have made possible world-wide conversation. The Americas have taken the lead in the international use of the telephone. As early as 1938, through a combination of radio, cables, and land-transmission lines, the United States could reach every continent and the major islands of the sea by means of seventy-four different telephone circuits.

In transportation of raw materials and manufactured goods and in communications, the world has moved toward an international order. In fact, we find a rather paradoxical situation in which we have international traffic and communication rules but national ownership and national control over the final decisions. The isolationism that has become linked to sovereign nationalism stands in sharp contrast with the interdependence of economic structure and functions.

An outstanding example of what are probably long-run trends in the pressures exerted by economies on governments is the consolidation of Western Europe under the European Common Market. Since 1955, industrial growth within the Common Market countries has averaged about 7 per cent per year—three times that of the United States. With less than half the land area of the United States, these countries in 1960 had a combined Gross National Product equal to 60 per cent of this country's GNP. They had 80 per cent more population than the United States, produced 10 per cent more steel, and held gold reserves worth 90 per cent of the United States gold reserve. Already, the short-run success of the Common Market has given rise to pressures in the United States for the lowering of international trade barriers.

The Spread of Self-Government

The diffusion of Western European patterns of culture around the world has had political consequences, which are continuing today. The colonial patterns of the eighteenth and nineteenth centuries brought more than technology to Africa, Asia, and Latin America; they also brought ideas.

Intentionally or unintentionally, colonial administrators, missionaries, traders, and settlers taught the natives of those continents many of the values of European cultures. We know enough about the integration of institutions not to expect Asians or Africans to imitate our economic sys-

One of the key problems confronting Africa, and a major reason for the large number of military coups, is the slow economic progress being made in many of the newly independent countries. The maps and charts here illustrate some of the problems.

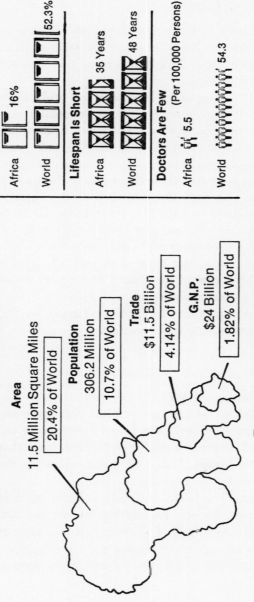

Continent is scaled according to its percentage of the world's area, population, trade and gross national product.

Area
11.5 Million Square Miles
20.4% of World

Population
306.2 Million
10.7% of World

Trade
$11.5 Billion
4.14% of World

G.N.P.
$24 Billion
1.82% of World

Literacy Is Low

Africa 16%

World 52.3%

Lifespan Is Short

Africa 35 Years

World 48 Years

Doctors Are Few
(Per 100,000 Persons)

Africa 5.5

World 54.3

FIGURE 11. Medicine, Literacy, and Economic Development in Africa
SOURCE: *The New York Times*, March 6, 1966, p. E4. © 1966 by The New York Times Company. Reprinted by permission.

tem, adopt Western notions of education, and so on without changing their political norms. The colonial powers may have done a better job than they intended of convincing their subjects that Western culture is superior to that of the natives; throughout Asia and Africa today there is a remarkable enthusiasm for adopting not only our technology but also at least the forms of our political institutions as well. As Figure 11 shows, however, many of the new nations are far behind the West in technologies ranging from medicine to literacy, and their poverty in international trade and GNP makes it hard for them to catch up.

In 1950 there were only four independent states in the entire Continent of Africa: Egypt, Ethiopia, Liberia, and the Union of South Africa. From 1950 through 1960, twenty-two new nations emerged in Africa. Almost all that is left of a vast European colonial empire are the Portuguese possessions of Angola and Mozambique, and they are torn by nationalistic uprisings.

At its inception in 1945, the United Nations had fifty-one members. Today 122 nations belong, and with the increase in membership Afro-Asian nations have become a majority.

Economic Position and Political Persuasion: American Trends

In many countries of the Western world, including the United States, there is a fairly close relationship between economic status and political party affiliation. Although there are many exceptions, in general, the higher one's occupational prestige in this country, the more likely he is to favor the Republican Party; the lower his occupational prestige, the more likely he is to believe that his interests are best represented by the Democratic Party.

This set of beliefs is carried into the polling booth. People tend to vote by stratum as well: Republican if upper class, Democratic if lower class. Approximately one-fifth of all business and professional people ordinarily vote Democratic. Only about one-tenth of unskilled workers usually vote Republican. Public-opinion research indicates that, in the average congressional election, Republicans can count on only one voter in four in northern cities larger than 500,000 people, one in eight among Negroes and Catholics, and one in five among northern manual workers.

A state with more than 20 per cent of its labor force unionized is likely to have relatively liberal governors and congressmen. States with less than 10 per cent of the labor force in unions are usually characterized by traditions both of conservative state administration and of sending conservative legislators to Congress.

The fact that there is a marked association between economic status and political affiliation was documented in the information gathered by the subcommittee of the United States Senate that investigated expenditures in the 1956 national election campaign. People with corporate interests, as well as those with labor interests, tended to have definite ideas about which party best represented those interests. The Republican Party received donations largely from people with big-business investments, whereas financial aid from organized labor went almost entirely to the Democrats.

As radio and television costs have constituted the larg-

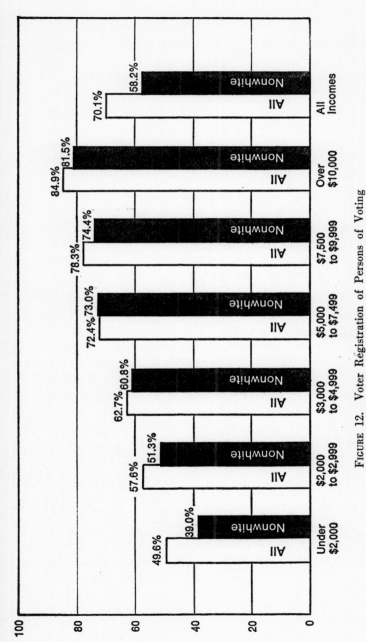

FIGURE 12. Voter Registration of Persons of Voting Age by Family Income, Color, and Sex for the United States, November 1964

SOURCE: U.S. Department of Commerce, Bureau of the Census, *Current Population Reports*, Series P-20, No. 143.

est single item of expenditure for both parties in recent presidential election campaigns, it is clear that greater wealth gives a candidate greater opportunity to plead his case before the electorate. To the extent that the mass media are molders of public opinion, wealth is political power.

There may be a trend away from voting by economic position. Figures from recent elections suggest that income, occupation, religion, and education are less directly related to voting behavior than they have been in the past. But it is not yet possible to tell whether or not this finding means a large-scale change in class-related political behavior. At any rate, as Figure 12 shows, there remains a sharp correlation between economic position and political activity, as indicated by registration and thus eligibility to vote.

The Boundaries of Behavior

Our emphasis on the role of the state should not obscure the importance of those governing structures that lie outside the realm of government and politics. Indeed, historically men have engaged in a running debate concerning activities properly subject to public control and functions that should be governed by the private sector of social life. The so-called free enterprise system maintains a dialogue with the state on what is private and what is within the domain of public control. In any society, much of the maintenance of internal order is a product of social controls that reside in institutions other than government.

Every society operates under some set of rules. Every group has certain regulations that its members learn. On the basis of what they have learned, individuals are able to predict the behavior of their fellows well enough to get along as members of the social order.

Most people learn the basic rules so well that, under ordinary circumstances, they are not even aware of them. One example of a relatively minor set of expectations will serve to illustrate the fact that societies could not operate if their cultures did not provide grounds for anticipating the behavior of the members in specific circumstances. When you approach a green traffic light, you proceed, confident that people traveling perpendicular to your course are facing a red light and will stop. You do not *know* that the light in other directions is red at this place and at this time; you *assume* it. You do not know the people approaching you at ninety-degree angles; you have never personally made arrangements with them assuring you that they will stop at red traffic signals. But you have learned that you have a right to expect the municipal government to keep the light in proper repair and to wire it so that when it is red facing one direction it will be green at right angles to that direction. You have learned that you have a right to expect people to stop when the signal is red in their direction, that you have an obligation to stop when it is red in your direction, and that you and others who violate these expectations will be punished.

Such norms are group-shared expectations. A pattern of expected behavior can be associated either with a certain situation or with a given position. The existence of such expectations is reflected in such statements as "Who ever heard of eating peas with honey?" "A Scout is courteous," "A gentleman pays his debts," or, more generally, "He shouldn't have done that." One is supposed to be quiet and respectful and not to interrupt others in a house of worship. This expectation is associated with a situation, whoever the participants may be. A lawyer has privileged communications—that is, he need not give the court damaging evidence against his own client. This expectation is associated with a position in the social structure.

Of course, not everyone in any society abides by all the norms all the time, and no norm is always obeyed. If everyone always did the "right" thing at the "right" time and place, there would be no need to have rules or laws.

Moreover, it is clear that not all norms—or even most of them—are legalized and codified. Most of the understandings that we share with other members of our society are informal. There is no law stating that one should not eat his peas with a knife, that men should hold doors open for women, that one should lend money to friends but not to strangers, or that one shakes hands when introduced. Yet we have all learned these expectations; they are part of our culture, and most of us conform to them most of the time.

The most obvious way to determine the importance of a norm for the members of a society is to observe how severely they punish those who violate it. Some norms are not looked upon as greatly important—they can be violated without severe punishment.

Adult males should wear coats and ties to church. People should arrive on time for appointments. Men may wear their hair crew cut; ladies should not. People should not park their automobiles in zones labeled "No Parking." Grade-school children should not call their teachers by their first names. One should not persistently make loud noises late at night in a residential area. People should not smoke in a chapel. One should bathe frequently enough so that others are not conscious of his body odors.

A man should not strike a woman. People should eat three meals a day. A person should respect his parents.

Each of the sentences in the preceding paragraph is a statement of a group-shared expectation, or norm, in contemporary American society. Some are covered by formal laws; others are not. Violations of some would be met by fines, imprisonment, or dismissal from one's job; failure to abide by others would be punished only by verbal statements of disapproval or by ostracism. All the listed norms have one thing in common, however: They are not looked on by most people as moral matters. People who smoke in chapel are regarded as crude but not immoral. People who are persistently late for appointments are considered thoughtless; they are not viewed as sinners. People who disturb the peace are a nuisance, not lost souls. We may avoid people who do not bathe frequently, but we do not judge them to be wicked. You may be fined for leaving your car in a no-parking area, but nobody will think a devil inspired you to park there.

Violators are considered boorish or careless or thoughtless, not evil. The rules cited are those that most people in the society expect most other people in the society to obey most of the time. They are deemed the "right" way, and "normal" people accept most of them unquestioningly. One can, however, challenge such a rule and suggest that it would not really be harmful to individuals or society to alter it, without being judged a social menace. Herein lies the difference between these customs and the mores.

Mores and norms are part of the culture, patterns of behavior that members of the society have learned to share and to expect from one another. But they differ from the folkways that we have been discussing in the importance attached to them and, consequently, in the severity of the punishment meted out to violators.

The mores generally are not open to question (although some of them are questioned by a few). In learning his culture, the individual so thoroughly internalizes the mores that he seldom consciously thinks of them as rules. The professor may be so irked at his warm academic robes that he toys with the idea of going to commencement in a T-shirt, but it will not occur to him to go in the nude. Law-enforcement agencies might take seriously a suggestion from a traffic authority for a set of graduated penalties for parking offenses: only a warning the first time, a small fine the second, a larger fine for the third violation, and suspension of the driver's license for the fourth offense. No one would take seriously a similar plan for dealing with murderers. Murder is a violation of the mores, and there is no disposition either to treat it lightly or, for that matter, to discuss whether or not it should be considered a violation of the mores.

Probably the best evidence of how thoroughly we internalize the mores is the difficulty most people would have in thinking of examples. Many general maxims that spring to mind are not mores. Taking a human life, for instance, is not necessarily a violation of the mores—it depends on who does it and under what circumstances. On some occasions our society gives medals, rewards, and public acclaim to those who take human lives. A hero's treatment is accorded the policeman who kills a wanted criminal in a gun battle. Many motion pictures portray heroes who, in the course of the story, violate the injunction "Thou shalt not kill." A storekeeper will not be punished for shooting a burglar in his store. Neither the law nor the mores prohibit killing in self-defense. Unintentional killing is not criminal unless it is the result of negligence on the part of the killer. In other words, to say that society prohibits the taking of a human life is far too broad a statement; it must be modified by a lengthy list of exceptions and qualifications.

Although we have laws to deal with murder, some of our mores are assumed to be so well learned that no law is needed to enforce them. The rare violations are met by community rejection and expressions of loathing for the participants and, if legally catalogued at all, are treated as "indecency" or "disturbance of the peace." Moral imperatives of this magnitude are so deeply impressed upon the members of society that most individuals cannot remember how or when they came to learn that certain behavior is wrong. Incest is an example of such a prohibition. Most people do not know when or from whom they learned that incest is morally evil, but a father who had sexual relations with his daughter would arouse in them a deep feeling of revulsion and contempt.

Similarly, if asked to cite a major prohibition of our society, most people would not think of mentioning the sharing of public toilet facilities at the same time by men and women (a common practice in many countries). That is to say, the prohibition is so efficient that the practice is literally unthinkable. If challenged, most citizens could not give a brief, rational explanation of why such behavior is wrong in the way that they would explain that it is wrong to violate a traffic regulation because it endangers the lives of others. They would be more likely to say, "Just because" or "Everybody knows it's wrong." It is, in other words, part of the mores.

In most relatively complex societies we find some kind of

political order as an over-all seat of power and authority in which law becomes an important norm of control. Laws are laid down to establish or maintain the rights, duties, and liberties of the members of the state. Rights imply a two-sided relationship, in which one person owes the other a duty, and the other person benefits thereby. A person has rights only insofar as others have duties toward him. One's rights set limits on other people's liberties. Freedom and responsibility always go together. In complex societies, the law represents the most certain of all the social norms.

Law, Government, and Individual Beliefs

The relation of the national community or public to the government—at least under democracy as we know it—is characterized by a number of important theories and practices. The core of these is stated in what we call the "Bill of Rights," including the rights of free speech, free assembly, petition, trial by jury, the writ of habeas corpus, and a number of others.

The mere fact that the Bill of Rights is the law of the state does not mean, of course, that its provisions are known and accepted by all citizens. As a matter of fact, research indicates that even most college students are not familiar with its provisions. Furthermore, when students were given an opinion questionnaire about the provisions of the first ten amendments to the Constitution without being told the source of the questionnaire items, most of them indicated disagreement with some of the provisions, and a majority disagreed with several of the amendments. Despite this demonstrated lack of information about the Constitution, when they were asked whether or not they agreed with all the provisions in the Bill of Rights, an overwhelming majority of the students replied in the affirmative.

Here we begin to approach the topic of sense of purpose as it relates to the political order. A sacred document like the Bill of Rights carries psychological weight whether or not people are familiar with the details of its contents. The Bill of Rights is associated in the minds of citizens with the Constitution, the Declaration of Independence, the idea of democracy, the Founding Fathers, and so on. It serves as an argument-clincher. A man watching a congressional investigation on television in a tavern may announce: "Fifth Amendment! They ought to jail him." But if his companion retorts, "He's allowed to do that—it's in the Constitution," that settles it. The disgruntled citizen may still feel that the witness belongs in jail, but he will not argue that we should violate the Constitution to put him there.

Among freshman and sophomore students taking social-science courses, I distributed a questionnaire in which the guarantees of the Bill of Rights were masked by paraphrase. They were asked to indicate their agreement or disagreement with them. A large majority of the students (about 72 per cent) disagreed with the Fifth Amendment's prohibition of double jeopardy (". . . nor shall any person be subject for the same offense to be twice put in jeopardy of life or limb . . ."), and a smaller majority (67.5 per cent) disagreed with the Sixth Amendment's guarantee that the accused shall be confronted by his accuser. Other guarantees "won" by disappointing majorities (only about 56 per cent favored the Fifth Amendment's guarantee that one must not be compelled to testify against himself). On the reverse side of the questionnaire, the students were asked to indicate what the questionnaire was about and, if they knew, to identify the source of the statements. Most of them did not answer at all; a number of them said that they concerned "government and ethics" or "the political rights of the people." Evidently, most of them did not recognize the Bill of Rights when they read excerpts from it.

But what is the sociological significance of widespread ignorance of laws basic to the governing of our society? As most of the students in this study failed to recognize the Bill of Rights, does that mean that they will not respect its provisions? If many citizens disagree with the Fifth Amendment's prohibition of double jeopardy or with the Sixth Amendment's guarantee of the right to confront one's accuser, does it mean that they will not obey the law? It does not, because the very fact that a social rule is enacted into law causes most people to respect it. The law itself carries weight, and it is therefore possible for men to enact laws and have those laws mold public opinion.

The traditional position of many sociologists has been that the mores and community opinion precede law, and their classic illustration has been the Eighteenth Amendment ("You can't legislate morality"). Many in the present generation of sociologists have moved to the position that, although morality cannot be legislated in a democracy in the sense of enforcing law to which the majority stands opposed, legislation *can* guide the development of community opinion on matters regarding which the bulk of the citizenry has not taken a strong stand one way or the other. An act outlawing reading cannot be enforced and will not be obeyed, because most people believe that they have a right to read and that the right is inalienable. On the other hand, a law forbidding the manufacture, sale, or use of sulphur matches could probably be enforced simply because of public indifference in this matter. In other words, the tendency of most people is to obey the law if it does not run counter to some strongly held value.

Indeed, law can itself help to shape cultural values. When Congress says that racial discrimination is illegal, people who might otherwise force Negroes to sit in the back of the bus or refuse to serve Negroes in restaurants may cease to discriminate because they do not want to break the law. They will then rear a generation of children who, unlike their parents, do not take racial discrimination for granted but, on the contrary, assume that racial discrimination is a bad thing.

A Crucial Question for Americans

How can our government accomplish its numerous and complicated tasks without becoming removed from the people and ceasing to be our government?

The norms of representative democracy prescribe that the state shall not be identical or coterminous with the society in which it is embedded. Under this theory, in the words of the usual Fourth of July oration, "The state is the servant, not the master, of the people." The theory means, in brief, that ultimate power in a democratic society rests with the citizens, not with the state. When we call a democracy "representative," we mean just that. Individuals "represent" the members of the national society and, in the last analysis, are responsible to them.

Because our government is a representative one, Americans have tended to seek political solutions for social problems. When tasks are not accomplished by private action, we delegate them to the public sector, to be taken care of by public action. This policy has contributed to the fact that the percentage of government employees in the total labor force has jumped from less than 3 per cent a century ago to more than 15 per cent today.

As we plot the historical trend, the only reasonable projection is that government will become larger and more powerful in the future. With the projected growth in our GNP, government revenues will increase by billions of dollars. As we have seen, foreign aid and international trading programs are subjects of increasing concern to businessmen; the very portion of the electorate traditionally most resistant to governmental intervention in the economy —the business community—is now urging the Federal government to help it adjust to European economic development and to the emergence of new nations. Our commitment to space exploration virtually assures that the cost of government will take at least as large a proportion of our national income a decade hence as it does now —and probably a larger share.

Big government does not automatically mean tyranny. The problem of governmental size and complexity rests in the difficulty of maintaining an informed electorate. One factor operating in our favor, of course, is the increasing amounts of education our citizens are receiving. It should be harder to practice the basest demagoguery on a constituency of college graduates than on a public of barely literate voters. But a serious hazard, if we want a population capable of passing informed judgment on the activities of its public servants, is the growth of secrecy in government and the growing acceptance by the public of the need for secrecy.

The classification of government documents as secret has become so routine that, according to testimony before the House government-information subcommittee, more than 1 million Federal employees are empowered to classify information. In other words, one American in every 180 can withhold from his fellow citizens information on the workings of their government.

William J. Lederer reports that pictures of plush furnishings in military transport planes, requested by Representative Daniel J. Flood, were stamped "secret," and then the Congressman's letter requesting the information was itself classified "secret." Representative Flood said, "It appears to me that this classification is designed to protect bureaucrats from embarrassment and not to protect the military secrets from potential enemies of the country."

In the study of belief in the Bill of Rights among university students, more than two-thirds of the students disagreed with the provision in the Sixth Amendment to the United States Constitution that guarantees the accused the right to confront his accuser. They felt that there were cases in which the government needed to use anonymous informers and that the government's need for secrecy was more important than the individual citizen's rights guaranteed in the Constitution.

If our government is to remain representative, we cannot subordinate the citizen's right to be informed to a mania for security. If free access to information cannot be the rule in a society, then representative government is doomed in that society.

CHAPTER 7

The American Dream
and the American Dilemma

One need not affiliate himself with a religious organization
in order to survive. But everywhere men believe in something that imbues them with a sense of purpose, be it
science, religion, or philosophy. An explanation of reality
is a part of every culture, and the student of society must
take that explanation into account if he is to understand
the nature of social life.

The sense of purpose is taught to people and maintained
in them by a variety of groups. Because of the range of
cultural variability, sociologists use the word "religion" in
a considerably broader sense than that of its ordinary
definition. For one person, a belief that the scientific

130

method offers the possibility for a better life in this world may serve this function; for another, the belief that service to a supernatural being promises a blissful and eternal afterlife may serve the same function.

Whether they occur in a church, a fan club, or a Marine Corps platoon, some values are available in every society with which the individual can identify. Such values offer him something to participate in and believe in and allow him to convince himself that his behavior is purposive, that his efforts are not in vain.

The American Dream

A discussion of purpose in American society is hardly identical with an analysis of formal religious participation. Although church membership and formal worship are important buttresses for the sense of purpose of many Americans, there are obviously other important sources of belief. After all, most Americans seldom enter a church. Even for those whose church activities are a central organizing force in their lives, participation in religious groups accounts for a relatively small portion of their time.

What binds Americans together into a society? What accounts for an awareness among them of shared goals and a common fate? What motivates Americans to make sacrifices so that their society will survive? What, in short, do Americans mean when they speak of defending "the American way of life"?

They are referring to a complex of values of which the Judaeo-Christian tradition is a part, but only a part. These cherished values also include individual freedom, political equality, and economic opportunity. They include the perhaps fundamental American belief that is at the core of the sense of purpose in the United States: that each individual has the right and indeed the obligation to improve himself and to better his position.

No other large contemporary nation places greater emphasis than does the United States upon the desirability of improving one's position. Ours is a loose class structure. Its boundaries are vague. Although barriers to mobility vary greatly from group to group, neither law nor custom prevents movement in the hierarchies of education, income, and occupation. American culture not only allows mobility; it encourages it.

Americans have proclaimed the ideals of equality of opportunity and freedom to achieve. The goal of success is a part of the fabric of American society. We honor the person who rises from humble origins to a position of power, wealth, and fame. We not only believe that there ought to be equality of opportunity; we also believe that, to a large extent, the United States does offer equality of opportunity. It therefore seems justifiable to look with disapproval on people who fail educationally or economically and to scorn those who make no attempt to better themselves. Our belief in the existence of opportunity and the desirability of success is so strongly entrenched that most Americans believe not only that each individual has the right to succeed but even that it is his moral duty to do so.

The religious institutions of a society play an important part in justifying its social structure. The moral system of the early Roman Catholic Church stressed otherworldliness, emphasizing rewards in the hereafter. The culturally established Catholic ethic of medieval times urged each man to accept his "calling"—that is, to do the best possible job in the status in which he found himself. If he was a serf, it was because God had intended him to be so, and he was as surely engaged in the Lord's work digging potatoes as he would have been ruling an empire. The rationale for the performance of worldly tasks was other-worldly: reparation for sins and purification through humility. This belief helped to sustain a set of norms suited to a caste-like social structure—as among the Hindus, medieval Christians were encouraged to make the best of the ascribed statuses into which they were born, on the ground that they would be rewarded for the acceptance of their worldly lot when they were reborn.

The Protestant Reformation changed this value structure by emphasizing the importance of work. Protestantism was a morality of individualism, and the individual was to be judged not on his humility but on the basis of what he accomplished. Calvin made virtues of industry, thrift, and self-denial. Wesley preached that the fruits of one's labor were the signs of salvation. The culmination of the Protestant Reformation, then, was to give divine sanction to the drive to excel.

It should not be assumed that the expression "Pro-testant Ethic" implies that people in contemporary Ameri-can society who are reared in the Protestant faith are taught to accept the mobility ethic whereas American Roman Catholics and those of other religions are not. "Protestant Ethic" is simply a phrase applied to a cultural value associated historically with the Reformation and the rise of capitalism; the concept has become part of the American ethos, and research indicates that American Jews and Catholics, as well as Protestants, internalize it.

In the same manner that religion has aided the Hindus to interpret the rigidities of their caste system, religion has provided moral justification to Americans for certain aspects of the American competitive class system—particularly the high premium placed on success and the consequent penalization of failure. Without this interpretation the successful might feel guilty about their success and the unsuccessful discouraged and resentful about their failures. Furthermore, given positive attitudes to the material world, it is not enough to claim that all moral imbalances will be rectified in heaven: it is crucial to interpret success as morally right—and failure as implying moral lack—here and now.*

Political, economic, and religious institutions all buttress the idea in the United States that upward mobility is a good thing.

The American Opportunity

This emphasis on the possibility for achievement in the United States derives partly from our peculiar situation as a young nation offering the combination of enormous natural resources and the opportunity to gain refuge from tyranny. First of all, this country afforded tremendous economic opportunities for the ordinary man—free land for settlement, other natural resources for easy exploitation, and a rapidly expanding business economy. Second, political freedom was an essential tenet almost from the beginning of our country, and it became increasingly significant as our population expanded under favorable material conditions. Third, religious tolerance and freedom not only furnished an outlet for individual choice

* Elizabeth K. Nottingham, *Religion and Society* (New York: Random House, 1954), p. 74.

134

but also gave our democracy a strong, supporting, non-economic, and nonpolitical ideology and practice. Finally, freedom of research and invention, freedom of personal migration, and other associated features of individualism and liberalism became deeply embedded in our culture.

In addition to these historical circumstances and cultural values, there are several characteristics of the American social structure that help to account for the high rate of upward mobility.

The millions of immigrants who entered the United States in the late nineteenth and early twentieth centuries made a certain amount of upward mobility virtually automatic for the people already here. Mass immigration increased the size of the population dramatically and thus contributed to a growth of the economy. Such growth meant that there was an increase in the number of occupational positions that had to be filled at all levels in the stratification structure. The filling of the lowest positions by immigrants (and by Negro Americans) working as low-paid unskilled laborers allowed native white Americans and their sons to move up the occupational structure.

Immigration is less important now than it has been historically as a factor in the rate of vertical mobility in the United States. Yet, despite legislation that has greatly slowed its rate, there is still a steady stream of immigrants entering the United States from other countries in the Western Hemisphere. Furthermore, the internal migration from rural areas to urban centers, particularly the movement of Negroes from the South to the North, has much the same effect on the total stratification structure that immigration used to provide.

Some of this internal migration is symptomatic of another factor that has contributed to a high rate of upward mobility in American society: technological change. The constant trend toward replacing human muscular effort with machinery, culminating in what we call "automation," has reduced the proportion of occupational positions that call for unskilled labor and has increased the number of semiskilled jobs. With this development have come the growth of large-scale industrial organizations and the expansion of government services; both kinds of bureaucracy require more white-collar personnel. Finally, the freeing through mechanization of larger and larger proportions of the labor force has allowed the expansion of service industries.

Some differentiation is a prerequisite to stratification: A class structure emerges only when there is some occupational specialization. There is some evidence, however, suggesting that as occupational specialization becomes more and more elaborate, it may contribute to a compression of the class structure. Any specialized learning is a kind of quasi magic; it gives one power over others who do not have the information. Thus, from the earliest days of priesthood and laity until very recently, a basic variable in most class systems has been literacy.

What happens when almost everyone is a specialist? Almost any specialization removes one from the bottom stratum of the unskilled. Since 1900, agricultural employment in the United States has fallen from 37.5 per cent to only 6.3 per cent of the labor force. The percentage of nonfarm laborers has dropped from 12.5 to 5.5 per cent. The creation of new, specialized occupations in the middle range of the stratification structure and the reduction of the number of occupations at the lower end of the structure necessitate some upward mobility. The social structure changes shape as fewer and fewer people are engaged in unskilled work and more and more enter semiskilled and white-collar statuses. One can argue that there is a tendency for the stratification pyramid of a society to become diamond-shaped with the increase of occupational specialization. For example, in traditional military organizations, the modal enlisted rank is private, and the least frequent is master sergeant; a diagram of the structure is a pyramid. But in a Strategic Air Command bomber squadron, with its electronics-maintenance specialists, there are more staff sergeants than privates, more technical sergeants than privates first class. A diagram of the distribution of enlisted rank approximates a diamond. That is, there is a contraction at the bottom of the pyramid as fewer and fewer people are engaged in unskilled work and an expansion in the middle as more and more people enter semiskilled and lower white-collar statuses. This means that, if every family had exactly enough children to take over the statuses the parents had occupied in the stratification structure, there would still be some upward mobility, for there would not be enough lower-class statuses for the children of lower-class people, and there would be more middle-class statuses than middle-class children to fill them.

Actually, people in each class do not have exactly the number of children needed to replace them in the class structure of the next generation. There are marked differences in the birth rates in the various income classes. People with family incomes of less than $3,000 a year have reproduction rates more than 50 per cent higher than those of families whose annual incomes are more than $5,000.

Professionals and other white-collar people typically do not have enough children to replace themselves in the labor force in the next generation. Farmers and farm laborers, on the other hand, have as much as 50 per cent more than enough children to take their places. This ratio would exist even if there were no changes in the number of people in each occupational category from generation to generation. Actually, we know that clerical and professional personnel have constituted an increasing proportion of the labor force, whereas unskilled laborers and farm laborers make up a smaller proportion of the total number of workers.

The openings created in the stratification structure by the low birth rates of the white-collar classes must be filled almost entirely (there is some "downward skidding") by the children of farmers and manual workers. Differential fertility, like mechanization and immigration, thus induces a certain amount of vertical mobility.

How much mobility is there in the United States? Do most people have a chance to better themselves? Or is the American class structure, as Vance Packard and others have charged, becoming more rigid with the passage of time?

The American Record

The success ethic, the belief that upward mobility is both possible and desirable in our society, has probably led to an exaggeration of the number of cases in which the poor laborer's son becomes president of the corporation. A study comparing more than 8,000 top executives in the largest firms in the United States in 1952 with the top business leaders in 1928 shows that, in both periods, more than 50 per cent of the business leaders were sons of owners or executives.

Not all occupations exhibit as high a rate of intergenerational continuity as business management. Most of the research on occupational mobility suggests that approximately two-thirds of the sons have been vertically mobile, either upward or downward, from the class strata of their fathers. Occupational mobility, then, is twice as likely as occupational continuity.

More important in evaluating the "rags to riches" myth is the fact that, although many sons experience *some* mobility, very few experience much. They move, but not far. If one is not in the same occupational category as his father, the next most likely place for him is in the occupational category either immediately above or immediately below that of his father. If a semiskilled worker in a mass-production factory has a son who is mobile, that son is most likely to move one step down to unskilled work or one step up to skilled labor; it is unlikely that he will become an executive or a professional man. In summary, more sons are vertically mobile than are not, but most sons work at either the same occupational level or one immediately adjacent to that of their fathers.

In the light of the effects of immigration, mechanization, and differential fertility on the openness of the class structure, it is not surprising that there is more upward than downward mobility. One study of the mobility of a representative sample of white urban males showed that nearly 30 per cent of the sons of manual laborers moved up into nonmanual occupational statuses, whereas fewer than 20 per cent of the sons of fathers in nonmanual work moved down into manual occupations. The point that most mobility is into adjacent strata still holds: Sons of manual laborers who move up into white-collar work are more likely to become salesmen or clerical workers than professional men or business executives.

Despite the considerable mobility between white-collar and the so-called "blue-collar" occupational statuses, the line between them is the greatest hurdle in the class structure. There is more mobility among the manual strata and among white-collar categories than there is between the two.

Studies of the mobility experienced by individuals during the time they are in the labor force point in general to the same conclusions as do intergenerational studies. They reveal more mobility than stability, but the bulk of the mobility is horizontal rather than vertical, occurring within occupational categories, not between them. Although it is not unusual for a person to change his occupation four or five times during his career, about half these moves are from one semiskilled job to another or from one managerial post to another and so on. Those shifts that do involve vertical mobility are usually limited in extent, the commonest pattern being a move to an immediately adjacent occupational category in the class structure. Career moves from the bottom to the top of the occupational hierarchy are as exceptional as is intergenerational mobility of this type. Research on career mobility further confirms the studies of intergenerational movement in suggesting that the balance is in keeping with the mobility ethic—for there is *slightly* more upward mobility than downward mobility.

Some social scientists have argued that the mobility ethic might become a norm inconsistent with the facts of the American class structure. They have said that the rate of upward mobility has been declining, that the strata are becoming more rigid. Certainly one can point to trends that suggest that the chance to work one's way up in American society is diminishing: the passing of the frontier days of free homesteading, the decline in immigration, the lower disparity in fertility rates among the different classes. As early as 1948, however, Edward Shils pointed out that "In spite of the oft-asserted claim that opportunities for ascent into the upper strata are diminishing in the United States, no conclusive evidence has been presented on either side of the issue by social research."*

Since that time, a considerable amount of research has been published on trends in social-mobility rates in the United States. These studies certainly offer no evidence to support the assertion that the American class structure is becoming more rigid. Indeed, even allowing for the expansion of opportunities for upward mobility as a result of the movement away from a class pyramid and toward a diamond-shaped class structure, the most thorough study to date concludes that the rate of upward mobility was about the same in 1940 as it was in 1910. If this conclusion is correct, even without counting the mobility that is an automatic result of changes in the occupational structure, then the actual mobility rate would seem to be higher now than it used to be. Warner and Abegglen, in research comparing the social origins of American business leaders in 1928 and 1952, conclude that American society is not becoming more caste-like. They find that the recruitment of business leaders from the bottom is taking

* Edward Shils, *The Present State of American Sociology* (New York: Free Press, 1948).

place now and seems to be increasing, especially in some
of the larger and newer firms. They conclude that mobility to the top is not decreasing but that, on the contrary,
between the Twenties and Fifties, at least, it was slowly
increasing.

A significant proportion of this mobility is traceable to
the impact of scientific technology on the economy. As
the importance of immigration and the frontier recede, the
slack is taken up by changes in the distribution of occupations and in amount of education, both induced by scientific advances and mechanization.

The American Dilemma

One of the sectors of American society that is experiencing extremely rapid change is the realm of majority-
minority relations. We are a nation founded by religious
and political minorities, and we are presently constituted
of racial, ethnic, and national minorities and their descendants. Over the years, the American melting pot has assimilated millions of people of diverse national and cultural
backgrounds who came to our shores as immigrants. But
we have not successfully assimilated our racial minorities.
Negroes, Orientals, and American Indians are not accepted
by many Americans as citizens with equal rights. This situation places a severe strain upon the American ethic of
equality of opportunity. Racial discrimination pinches our
pride in democracy, taints our dedication to the brother-
hood of man, and maims a motivational system based on
fair play for every citizen striving for success.

The massive social upheaval that we summarize under
the heading "desegregation" is a change in the rules of

social life in America. Our social order is rent by what Gunnar Myrdal called "an American dilemma": the conflict born of a contradiction between the mores calling for racial discrimination and those demanding equality of opportunity.

The Federal courts have insisted that "separate facilities are inherently unequal." The maze of "separate but equal" facilities is becoming useless as a place in which to hide from the social realities of the twentieth century. As more and more formal education is provided for each generation, some of the old myths about racial differences wither away. A gradually changing public opinion gives slaps of disapproval to hands clutching at old customs of color caste.

Social change always presents problems for individuals, and many Americans in the 1960s are more disturbed about desegregation than their grandparents were about female suffrage. Some react against the idea of equality of treatment of people of all races with an emotional violence comparable to that their ancestors displayed when faced with the idea that the sun rather than the earth was the center of the universe.

Most Americans have grown up in a world that taught by example that white skin was the center of the universe. Re-evaluating such beliefs threatens emotional security. Things that used to be known for sure become uncertainties. How is a white clerk in an exclusive shop supposed to behave when faced with a wealthy Negro customer? In the world the clerk grew up in there were no wealthy Negroes (or so he had assumed). What is a Negro sharecropper supposed to do when his minister urges him to register and vote? His parents taught him to pay attention to trustworthy leaders like his minister and to avoid trouble with whites; now he cannot do both. When white Americans know as an article of faith that having Negroes move into a neighborhood lowers property values because Negroes are shiftless, dirty, and uneducated, what are those white suburbanites to think when their new neighbor is neat, ambitious, a college graduate—and a Negro? The path to correct behavior is no longer clear; social expectations are ambiguous and poorly defined. And it is not just the fact of social change that makes life difficult; it is the rapid rate of that change.

As recently as 1950, only eighteen states prohibited segregation in transportation and recreation facilities. Now the Interstate Commerce Commission has outlawed all racial barriers on trains and buses and in terminals.

In 1950 there were more states in which segregation in the public schools was mandatory than there were states in which school segregation was prohibited. The Supreme Court outlawed public-school segregation in 1954. Today every state has begun at least token compliance with the order.

Twenty years ago the white primary prevented the majority of Negroes from voting in the elections that counted in the South. The Supreme Court struck at white primaries in 1954, and in 1957 Congress passed the first civil rights act in eighty years, empowering the Justice Department to bring suits to win the ballot for Negroes. The impact of legislation is clearly shown in Figure 13, which records the increase in Negro voter registration in five states within five months of the passage of the 1965 voting rights act.

In 1870, 80 per cent of all American Negroes could

Number of Negro Voters
(Thousands)

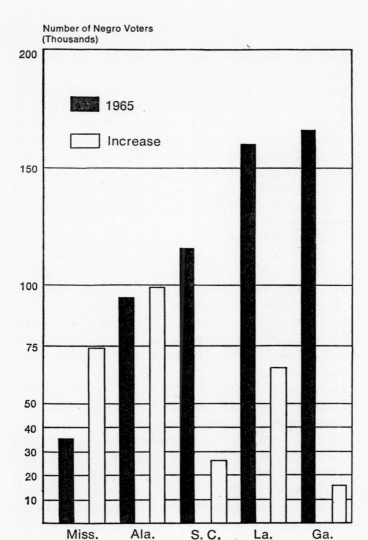

FIGURE 13. 1965 Negro Voter Registration in Five
States Prior to Passage of Voting Rights Act and
Increases, in Numbers, in Registration After Passage
SOURCE: For August 1965 figures, U.S. Department of Com-
merce, Bureau of the Census; for January 1966 figures,
U.S. Department of Justice.

neither read nor write. That illiteracy rate has been reduced to 7 per cent. The proportion of college graduates among young Negro adults has tripled in the past twenty years.

These objective changes in the status of the American Negro are important catalysts for change, but so is an emerging body of public opinion that is intolerant of intolerance. The National Opinion Research Center asked a national sample of white Americans in 1942 whether or not they believed that "Negroes are as intelligent as white people—that is, can they learn just as well if they are given the same education?" Only 42 per cent of the whites said "Yes." But by 1956, the proportion answering "Yes" to the same question had risen to 77 per cent. Another NORC survey asked white adults, "If a Negro with just as much income and education as you have moved into your block, would it make any difference to you?" In 1942, only a little more than one-third of the respondents said "No"; by 1956, the proportion was more than one-half.

Most striking for projecting what the future holds are research studies that tabulate responses according to age and amount of education. When the American Institute of Public Opinion asked a national sample of Americans, "If your party nominated a generally well-qualified man for President, and he happened to be a Negro, would you vote for him?" of those who had only a grade-school education, 49 per cent said "No." The percentage drops to 39 per cent for those who completed high school, and among those with college education only 21 per cent said they would reject a well-qualified candidate on grounds of race. A similar pattern emerges with age. Thirty-four per cent of the voters twenty-one through twenty-nine years old said "No." The percentage rose to 37 among those aged thirty-nine to forty-nine. The highest negative response was among people fifty years of age and over—48 per cent. Four out of five American youths now graduate from high school, and two of those go on to college. The youthful and the educated are a growing pressure group.

Research on desegregation by Melvin M. Tumin of Princeton University suggests that "the hard core" of Southern resistance to desegregation lies among the poor and uneducated. The outstanding characteristic of those most willing to resort to violence to defy the law of the land is a below-average amount of schooling. The violence-prone, "hard-core" people are as stable in residence patterns as are their neighbors; they belong to churches in about the same proportion and attend about as frequently. But their earning power is significantly lower than that of their neighbors, partly because a much smaller proportion of them have completed nine or more years of school. The wider society impinges much less directly upon them; they are less influenced by newspapers and magazines; they are less well prepared than their fellow citizens to adjust to rapid social change.

At present, the swift change in the social fabric wrought by desegregation seems to be concentrated in the South. This concentration makes change all the more difficult, for the South is characterized by the very elements that contribute most to resistance to change. The South remains predominantly agrarian, with a high birth rate and a low level of formal education. It is the most rural section of urban America, the least-schooled region in a highly educated society, a relatively unindustrialized portion of a technologically oriented nation.

But it is shortsighted to think of desegregation as a problem that is essentially the South's. There it is focused and at present causes the most disruption of living patterns. Remember that, fifty years ago, 90 per cent of all American Negroes lived in the states of the old Confederacy. One measure of the swiftness of the change in the Negro's status is that half of the Negro population now lives in the cities of the North and West: New York City is now 14 per cent Negro, Chicago 24 per cent, Philadelphia 26 per cent, Detroit 29 per cent, and Newark 35 per cent Negro. These tremendous migrations create problems at both ends of the line. Mississippi lost one-fourth of its total Negro population in the 1940s, and, although some Mississippians may laughingly claim that migration promises the ultimate solution of their problem at the North's expense, they are mistaken. It is the Negroes Mississippi can least afford to keep who stay at home: Those most likely to migrate are the young people with better than average education. And every year these people are packing into already overcrowded Negro ghettoes in the Northern cities, their residential segregation ensuring segregation in schools and other facilities.

A Negro boy in America today has about half the chance to complete high school that a white boy has; one-third the chance to complete college or become a professional man; one-seventh the chance of earning $10,000 a year; twice the chance of being unemployed. The average Negro college graduate will earn less in his lifetime than will the average white who never went beyond the eighth grade. A Negro American's life expectancy is seven years shorter than a white American's. In 1960, the median money wage was $3,058 for Negroes and $5,425 for whites. Only 39 per cent of white families earned less than $5,000; 71 per cent of Negro families had incomes below $5,000. And the relative gap between Negro and white family income has been increasing since the mid-Fifties.

With perhaps intentional irony, President Johnson described the race-relations situation in the United States admirably in his report on the 115 companies participating in President Kennedy's "Plans for Progress" hiring program: "Within those companies whose reports have been received, the ratio of white salaried employees to nonwhite dropped from 61 to 1 at the beginning of the reporting period to 60 to 1 at the end. We still have a long way to go."

In one shameful sense the demands of the civil-rights protest movement *are* revolutionary. The American Negro has been so disadvantaged economically and socially that a real attempt to bridge the gap would require a reallocation of resources that would indeed be revolutionary.

The problem of desegregation belongs to the whole country. The South at present is particularly vulnerable to rapid change, for the southern states depended for segregation on laws that have been declared unconstitutional. The North feels different pressures because its segregation is accomplished informally through residential patterns and is harder to strike at through the courts. But race relations is not a Southern problem; it is what Gunnar Myrdal called it: an American dilemma.

A Crucial Question for Americans

How can we maintain an open class structure and sustain the motivation of Americans to keep it open?

In all large societies, people classify one another and rank the resulting categories from higher to lower. The degree of definiteness or rigidity of the stratification structure varies considerably from society to society. In some societies, every member is born into a category. Under ordinary circumstances, he cannot change to another one; he must marry a person born into the same category as he; and his membership will be the prime determinant of his wealth, the amount of education he gets, the occupation in which he spends his life, and various other features of his social life. Strata as rigid as those described are called "castes." In other societies, the stratification structure is relatively vague and changeable. The United States is an example of such an open-class system, in which birth or lineage is not very important in the determination of class status. Such societies do not have classes that are discrete, well-defined units as are castes; their classes are simply aggregates of statuses that have approximately similar prestige.

The son of an accountant might quit high school, never go to college, become a garage mechanic, yet marry the daughter of his employer. Furthermore, there might be some disagreement among members of the community as to whether the accountant is upper class or middle class and whether the garage mechanic is middle class or lower class. The criteria by which people assign prestige to a status in modern urban-industrial societies are vague and shifting. Consequently, classes are not clearly delineated but tend to overlap and blur into adjacent strata. Actually, the ambiguity lies in the relative weights assigned to the different factors that contribute to an individual's class status. For example, there is consensus in the United

States that it is better to make much money than little, that it is better to be educated than ignorant, that professional occupations have higher prestige than unskilled work. But it is not so easy when more than one criterion is involved. Who ranks higher in the class structure, the person with a moderate income and a great deal of education or the one with a moderate amount of education and a high income?

Various occupations, incomes, and amounts of education lead people to share different norms and to behave differently. In other words, the existence of a class structure leads to the development of class subcultures. And in time the subcultures themselves become critieria of placement in the class structure. Not only one's income but the way he spends it, not only his occupational status, but his attitude toward it become factors in determining his class status.

The evidence of differences in style of life includes variations by class in sexual behavior, in family pattern, in religious participation, and in many other culture patterns. People in the lowest-income strata spend nearly three-fourths of their total incomes for food, whereas those in the higher strata spend less than one-fourth of their incomes for food. Obviously, lower-class families are left not only with less money but also with a lower *proportion* of their total incomes available for education and other expenditures that might improve their class positions. The smaller amount of money available for purposes other than groceries is reflected in the fact that lower-class people exceed those in wealthier classes both in symptoms of illness and in the proportion of those symptoms not being treated by physicians. Lack of money is likely to be only one of the factors accounting for this situation; lower education levels would make it less likely that the lower-income classes would be aware of the need for treatment of some symptoms.

The basic variables of class structure reinforce one another through the medium of life chances. People who have high income and college education are more likely to favor college education for their children. And those who receive college education are considerably more likely than are those who do not to be able to afford to send their children to college.

There is, then, an element of the self-fulfilling prophecy in vertical mobility. One reason for the high degree of occupational inheritance in business-leadership statuses is that businessmen's sons are taught to expect to fill these occupational statuses, whereas manual workers' sons learn that there is little chance of their attaining such positions. Indeed, young people with equally high I.Q.s show differences in their educational and occupational aspirations directly related to the occupational statuses of their fathers. The higher the prestige of the father in the hierarchy of occupational statuses, the more likely the son is to aspire to a high occupational status himself.

In the same way that race can become an ascribed status through the social definition imposed by the culture, so can education and occupation, and therefore income, be ascribed through class subcultures. This ascription of class characteristics constitutes a serious value problem in a society in which people believe in an open-class system, in equality of opportunity. The problem is doubly serious where race and class overlap. To the extent that Americans use "Negro" as a synonym for "lower class," they can be more comfortable in their patterns of discrimination against the less privileged.

If we look at what are called "races" in any given society as a culturally accepted definition of the situation, we can explain race relations as part of the distribution of power in the social structure. Dominant-minority interaction can be treated as a class situation or power distribution deemed desirable by privileged groups or categories. Those in power then find it socially convenient and normatively acceptable to explain the *status quo* as a consequence of hereditary differences.

The American stratification structure tolerated, within its open-class system, human slavery, which later, under military-political pressure, gave way to a semicaste system based on color. The persistence of the white-Negro caste relationship is not only a cultural paradox but also continues to present the United States with one of its most serious and pressing local and national dilemmas.

Throughout the United States, whites have been getting out of the bottom income bracket more rapidly than Negroes have, and a higher proportion of whites than of Negroes has been moving into the top income category. Furthermore, as can be seen in Table 2, the products of centuries of racial discrimination appear in the relationship between education and income. White Americans who have completed elementary school average higher lifetime earnings than do Negro Americans who are college graduates.

It is important to the maintenance of the American way of life that Americans implement their belief in equality of opportunity. The most effective way to ensure this belief is to minimize the roadblocks of class status, race, and

TABLE 2

Male Lifetime Earnings by Race and Education

(in thousands)

Highest Grade Completed	White	Negro	Negro as Percentage of White
Elementary School			
Less than 8 Years	$157	$ 95	61
8 Years	191	123	64
High School			
1 to 3 Years	221	132	60
4 Years	253	151	60
College			
1 to 3 Years	301	162	54
4 Years	395	185	47
5 Years or More	466	246	53
Average	241	122	51

SOURCE: U.S. Department of Labor, Bureau of Labor Statistics, *Employment and Earnings*, February 1964.

regional inequality and to make it possible for each individual to go as far as his talents and drive will carry him.

CHAPTER 8

The Conformity Question
and the Search for Talent

Ever since David Riesman added "inner-directed" and "other-directed" to the American lexicon, we have been asking one another whether or not there is too much conformity in American life. We worry that there is not enough encouragement of individualism, that we are too much a herd. We have, of course, a tradition of concern that we not be too much bound by social expectations; it has found expression from Henry David Thoreau to Sinclair Lewis. Still each new analysis of "the organization man" or of "mass culture" brings a fresh rash of sermons, seminars, and soul-searching.

What are the facts? Are Americans more conformity-oriented than are other peoples? Isn't conformity necessary for social survival?

Varieties of Nonconformity

The fact that a social group expects certain behaviors from an individual or from another group does not always mean that these expectations are met. No norm is *always* obeyed; no individual *always* conforms to every set of expectations.

There are several reasons why the behavior of a large number of people never conforms perfectly to the norms of the society in which they live. For one thing, norms are general, whereas an individual's behavior in any situation is specific. An expectation, if it is to apply to different people in varying situations over a period of time, must be stated in quite general terms. There are therefore always some situations in which the norm is not applicable. Each of us learns the rules of his society as a set of broad (and usually flat) generalizations: "You should eat meat with a fork, not with your fingers" or "Honor thy father and thy mother." But one can eat meat with his fingers at a picnic, and no one would expect a starving man to eschew food because he did not have a fork. Indeed, there are situations in which violation of the norm becomes itself an expectation: In many societies, the son whose father commits treason is expected to reject, not honor, his father.

The generalized nature of norms is only one factor that can help us explain deviation. Another is variation among individuals and groups in their perception of what the norms are and their interpretation of what they mean. It is possible, for reasons ranging from mental incompetence to geographic (and hence social) isolation, for a person to be unaware of some of the norms of his society. In American society, for example, an illiterate is cut off from an important source of information about what is expected of a citizen. Many Americans are aware of the norm "Keep the sabbath day to sanctify it, as the Lord thy God hath commanded thee," but there is widespread variation in the interpretation of this admonition.

Finally, one cannot understand the amount of deviance in a mass society without noting the extent to which it is the product of differing subcultures. Normative standards vary by social class, by ethnic group, by degree of urbanization, and by region. Is it proper to enter a store, sit down on the counter, and offer a chew of tobacco to the clerk? A group-shared expectation in a company store patronized by sharecroppers in rural Arkansas may be a violation of the norms in a Park Avenue gift shop catering to wealthy New Yorkers. Taking a hubcap from an automobile in a lower-class slum area is stealing; taking a piece of the wrought-iron picket fence (much more expensive than hubcaps) from in front of your neighbor's fraternity house at a college is only a high-spirited prank. In this case, class position determines what is or is not criminal.

Within the span of a generation, we have projected into urban life the majority of the Negro one-tenth of our population, many of whom were brought up to live in what amounted to feudal fiefdom. Although in education and other endeavors enormous strides are being made, enormous prices are also being paid for the suddenness of emancipation. As Philip M. Hauser points out:

Tossing an empty bottle on an asphalt pavement in the city has quite different consequences from tossing it into a cotton field. Using physical force, including a knife or gun, in the resolution of personal conflict receives much more attention and has a much greater impact on the community in the city than it had in the rural South. The patterns of family and sexual behavior which the Negro inherited as a product of his history and his share in the American way of life have created the many complications connected with the administration of Aid to Dependent Children, in the urban setting.*

In a multigroup society such as the contemporary United States, with its host of racial, ethnic, class, occupational, and regional subcultures, deviance is more than a little in the eye of the beholder.

Men behave in large part on the basis of what they believe to be true. It is interesting to note that biologists know that there are no pure races, but their knowledge will not explain the behavior of a racist. To understand the revulsion some people may feel about "race-mixing," you do not need to know biology; you need to know what those individuals believe.

Social facts are multiple facts. Unlike the three- (or four-) dimensional objects of physical space-time continua, social objects do not lend themselves to simple demonstrations of truth or falsity. This problem is not only a matter of insufficiently refined measurement in social science, as is sometimes supposed; it is inherent in the nature of society itself. That is, one's perception and definition of a social object depend, in part, upon his relation to that object. For example, a school principal can define a student as a "troublemaker," "hoodlum," or whatever; the

* Philip M. Hauser, *Population Perspectives* (New Brunswick: Rutgers University Press, 1960), p. 150.

student's father may see him as a "good boy," "gentleman," and so forth—*both* may be correct. The social scientist's problem is not to determine who is correct but rather to point out the institutional and cultural characteristics underlying those different interpretations of fact.

Nowhere is ethnocentrism more easily seen than in the attempts of people from different societies to understand one another's mores. Yet some societies will tolerate considerably more deviance than others. One of the outstanding differences between a folk community and an urbanized society is the degree to which urbanism not only allows but even necessitates the exercise of choice. In a folk society there is an accepted way, rooted in tradition, of dealing with both routine and critical situations. In an urban social environment there is a host of alternatives. As the city forces people to make choices, it forces the substitution of rational approaches for traditional ways of doing things.

The enforced rationalism of the city helps to encourage mechanical inventiveness, artistic creativity, political individualism, and the exercise of ingenuity and self-expression. In this sense, urbanism and industrialization serve each other as handmaidens. The great centers of learning, invention, art, and culture have historically been located in cities.

Urbanization gives rise to a great heterogeneity in the population. Urban life leads to ethnic and migrant differentiation and allows people with different skin color or language or religion to pass relatively unnoticed in a way that could never be possible in the primary organization of a folk community. In addition, the occupational specialties associated with the complex division of labor create differences in the population: variations in training, values, work hours, recreation patterns, and, ultimately in style of life.

An industrial society needs some of its nonconformists, for example, its artists, its critics, and its scientists. Science now provides us with a means of directing and even predicting many inventions.

What place has special ability or so-called inventive genius in invention? It is easy to assume that inventions are the result of the innate abilities of a few people. There is no doubt that, given the proper cultural stimulus, the stratum of superior individuals will furnish the inventors. Yet what the superior person will do with his capacity depends on the society and its culture. It is hardly conceivable that the genius of the jungle would become a great physicist, but he might well become a military leader or the inventor of a new religious ritual.

The absolute and relative number of first-rate minds will always be factors in scientific advancement as well. Suppose that all the "class A" nuclear physicists, men of superior native ability, should be wiped out at one stroke, with no replacements available. The "class B" men would still be capable of continuing important research and invention, for, with present techniques, worthy discoveries and valuable applications could still be made. But few doubt that long-range advances in physics would be slowed enough to affect all related scientific progress.

Furthermore, we often fail to recognize that the capacity to use and benefit from any invention or idea is a vastly different thing from the initiation of the idea. A man who cannot make a discovery may be able to apply it. So too there is little correlation between the first-rate ability needed for invention and application and the capacity to make use of an invention. A moron may learn to run a truck or even to make minor repairs, but he lacks the ability to understand the scientific laws on which the internal combustion engine is founded.

The inception and direction of invention depend, therefore, on culture, as well as on superior ability. The particular direction of inventions and their nature are determined by culture. Often we forget the slow accumulation of basic knowledge by less well-known men who make possible the more striking work that we hear about. The inventions of Thomas A. Edison in electricity, for instance, would have been impossible without hundreds of researchers in the century before him. The close relationship between cultural base, values and attitudes, and high abilities is well demonstrated by the large number of duplicate inventions and discoveries during the period of modern science.

Clearly, inventions and discoveries do not depend on exceptional individuals alone but on the nature of the culture out of which the new elements in the invention arise as well. True, if there were no superior people available to make inventions, the rate of invention would be retarded. But, as advances in invention depend so much on minor accretions to the total body of knowledge, it is indeed doubtful that any one particular inventor is essential at any given time. Great men alone do not make inventions, but neither can culture as a body of knowledge alone induce them.

Where does the United States stand? Does our culture enforce too much conformity for us to survive in an age of scientific inquiry? How are we doing at searching out our most talented citizens and equipping and encouraging them to act as innovators?

An American Appraisal

It is perhaps a healthy sign that so many Americans worry about whether or not there is too much conformity in our society, but there is something wryly amusing about it too. The people of the United States tolerate a range of behavior in their fellow citizens that the people of most societies throughout human history would have found simply incredible.

A young man or woman in America can marry or not, as he or she wishes. Marriages are not arranged by families or by tribal elders. Marriages can be performed by civil officials or by any of a host of clergymen of different faiths.

Parents can send their child to public school or to parochial school, as they wish. Once the child has received the required minimum number of years of schooling, he can continue or not, according to his abilities, his financial situation, and his personal desires.

A person is not even required to work, if he can get along without doing so. He is certainly not assigned a place in the labor force; he is allowed to work at any job he can obtain and hold, in the city or the country, in Idaho or Georgia. He can work day or night; he can have a part-time job or, if he wants, two jobs. He can spend most of his earnings to suit himself, and he is faced with the greatest array and variety of consumer goods ever available in human history. He is allowed to own his home if he is able to; he is not required to do so.

An American citizen can vote from a selection of candidates for office to govern him, any of whom can later be turned out of office by the citizens. He does not have to vote at all.

In substantial measure, he can do what he wants with his recreational time. Not only is he encouraged by billboards to attend the church of his choice; he is also free to choose not to attend any church at all. It is difficult for an American to realize that his ancestors were slaughtering one another only a few centuries ago for being affiliated with the "wrong" denomination of the Christian faith.

In short, ours is an urban, industrial society that defines as acceptable a wide range of behavior and that tolerates an enormous amount of deviance in familial roles, educational policy, economic behavior, political participation, and religious beliefs. But industrialization is not without its costs.

Industrialization has made possible the rapid interchange of persons and ideas not only within large societies but also among societies. Ultimately, this interchange could, through the development of a single life style, lead to a single human culture on earth. But that possibility, like the Second Coming, resides somewhere in the indefinite future. Meanwhile, the rapid interchange of persons and ideas increases, if only mathematically, the possibility of interpersonal and intergroup friction, both within and among societies.

Melvin Tumin lists as minimum characteristics of a "mass society" a set of factors that are virtually ideal for engendering conflict:

Traditional criteria of prestige, such as membership in exclusive kinship groups, are rapidly vanishing. . . . The "ideal"

values insist that existing lines of social differentiation, including class and caste barriers, are temporary, and in the long run,
insignificant; that all men are ultimately equal, some tempo-
rarily more equal than others; but that in some way we take
turns at being more equal, since this is a condition which is
theoretically available to everyone under the right happen-
stances. . . . It is theoretically permissible and even well-
mannered to compete with everyone, regardless of rank.*

Tumin's formulation makes conflict seem very likely.
So does T. H. Marshall's analysis of the requisites for
emergence of modern class structures in industrial societies. The core concept, according to Marshall, is citizenship, a status involving specified rights and powers. The
history of the social development called industrialization is
the story of the admission to citizenship of the new strata
produced by industrial societies. Citizenship has three
components—civil, political, and social—and access to
those components has become a crucial part of citizenship
in the eighteenth, nineteenth, and twentieth centuries,
respectively.

The bourgeoisie established in the eighteenth century
the civil rights of citizenship: liberty, the right to own
property, freedom of speech, and equality before the law.
With universal manhood suffrage, the working classes acquired in the nineteenth century the political rights of
citizenship: access to participation in the law-making and
decision-making processes. In the twentieth century, a
major component of the definition of citizenship for all is
social rights: education, security, and welfare.

As these citizenship rights spawned by industrialization

* Melvin M. Tumin, "Some Unapplauded Consequences of Social
Mobility in a Mass Society," *Social Forces*, 36 (October 1957), 33.

imply equality and as stratification is a system of inequality, conflict between class and citizenship is endemic in industrial social systems.

To put it another way, dynamic or open-class systems are more likely to be productive of conflict than are estate or relatively closed systems; status is more stable than is contract. As Marshall says:

> Some people hold that social mobility affords a safety valve and helps to avert the threatened conflict. Although this is true up to a point, I think its importance can easily be exaggerated. Where individual mobility is automatic, or nearly so, class loyalty develops with difficulty. If every apprentice has a reasonable hope of becoming a master he will form his associations on the basis of his trade or profession rather than of his social level. Again, where a whole group can rise in social estimation and economic value, leaving no stragglers, the alliance of groups into classes is more difficult. This is no doubt the effect of the recent rise of many skilled occupations into the ranks of the professions. But where mobility is individual and not automatic, but depends on the results of competitive striving, I am doubtful whether the same result follows. When the race is to the swift, the slow, who are always in a majority, grow tired of their perpetual defeat and become more disgruntled than if there were no race at all. They begin to regard the prizes as something to which they are entitled and of which they are unjustly deprived. They declare that no man ought to be made to race for his bread and buttter, and the argument is not without force. Especially is this so when society shows itself indifferent to the condition of the losers on the ground that the road to better things is ever open before them.[*]

With automation, we have made great strides toward freeing the individual worker from the deadening monot-

[*] T. H. Marshall, *Class, Citizenship, and Social Development* (Garden City: Doubleday, 1964), pp. 172–3.

ony of assembly-line work. With our political tradition of individual freedom and our cherished social value of offering each citizen a maximum opportunity for self-development, we have the building blocks for a social organization dedicated to the good of the whole.

What about our exploitation of the creative abilities of Americans? Are we taking advantage of the talents we have?

Social scientists have largely abandoned the concept of human ability as an innate, unchangeable characteristic. Research suggests that the upper limits of performance are seldom if ever reached by any individual, partly because experience contributes to the total amount of ability in each person, as can be seen in the case of the isolated child of the deaf-mute mother.

The achievements of American society in the sciences arise from the work of a relatively small number of highly educated scholars. It is estimated that our output of Ph.D. holders will nearly double in the next decade. This boom in formal education should provide a terrific impetus to our accumulation of knowledge.

Other social research suggests that we have overemphasized heredity in interpreting the relationship between the intelligence of parents and the achievements of their children. The richness of vocabulary that children absorb in the home influences their test scores and school success, and the warmth of family environment has been demonstrated to affect a child's concept of himself as competent, thus contributing to his motivation. When we consider these findings, it seems that raising the level of education of our whole population, as we are doing, and thus producing a generation of better-educated parents must necessarily increase the intellectual qualities of succeeding generations.

As Robert E. L. Faris said in his presidential address to the American Sociological Association:

> Men of wealth, position, and responsibility wishing to provide security for their children, find that there is actually no way of having absolute assurance that a fortune can survive. Currency can fluctuate in value and deteriorate through war and inflation. Gold and diamonds have arbitrary worth which can vanish with economic disorganization. Land can be taxed away or confiscated by agrarian reformers. No kind of material wealth is more secure than the social organization which stands back of it. The most favorable chance of survival, therefore, eventually goes to persons of highest general ability and wisdom who can deal with problems of complexity in a time of change. Effective intelligence, then, is a richer legacy than acres of diamonds, not only to the heirs of a tycoon, but also to the posterity of a nation. To learn how to expand the heritage of collective intelligence would create the best legacy we could leave to the children of our children.*

The application of the scientific method to a better understanding of our social system offers us our best chance for survival. More education and more understanding of human social ways must lead to greater appreciation of deviance and less pressure for conformity.

A mass society does not maintain its sense of purpose as a consequence of its having a mass focus of attention. A complex urban industrial social structure is not characterized by the unity of experience and interest known to a small tribe. Large societies must develop and maintain

* Robert E. L. Faris, "Reflections on the Ability Dimension in Human Society," *American Sociological Review*, 26 (December 1961), 843.

norms of at least minimal tolerance because, by the very nature of mass society, the individual member becomes attached to special purposes and personal goals. These purposes and goals are highly meaningful in his life but differ from those held and pursued by other individuals and groups. The cement that holds a mass society together is not that of mutuality, common purpose, and shared goals. The binding force is interdependence. It is for this reason that the solution of the American dilemma must be considered crucial for our social survival.

CHAPTER 9

Social Change
and Free Men

The five functions that a society must, at minimum, accomplish in order to survive are (1) to replace its personnel when they move out, die, or become unable to perform their tasks; (2) to teach new personnel what is expected of them and how to participate in the society; (3) to produce and distribute goods and services for its personnel; (4) to ensure a level of order such that its personnel are able to perform the essential functions and to protect them from outside attack; and (5) to motivate its members by providing and sustaining a sense of purpose at such a level that people will accomplish the other necessary functions.

These prerequisites for social organization and survival serve as a framework for this book; Chapters 3 through 8 examine the main drift of American society. We describe the major social trends in the United States in population and family structure, education, the economy, government, and the value system. Our intent, in charting social trends in each of these essential areas of human social activity, is to gain a perspective on and insight into the scientific revolution and industrialization in those areas of social life where their impact is most profound.

An orderly description of the direction of American society in replacing personnel, educating them, providing for them, maintaining order, and sustaining purpose should provoke ideas about issues and prospects. Each of the five preceding chapters closes with a crucial question confronting thoughtful Americans in a rapidly changing world. How can we reduce the rate of population increase? How can we provide people with an opportunity for as much education as they can use? How can a complex economy, with unprecedented concentration of power, be kept in the role of servant, rather than allowing its needs to dictate political policy and national purpose? Can a government be as big as that required by a huge industrial society and still be responsive to individual citizens and small groups, or is bigness necessarily the road to tyranny? In a multigroup, stratified society in which a person's social and economic background structures not only his access to rewards but also his motivation to strive for them, can we maintain an open class structure?

These questions, of course, are only a sample from the universe of value conflicts that are of concern to the educated citizen. Each social trend is accompanied by a new social challenge. Time and again we must choose between some value commitments and others on specific policy issues. Is the rate of population growth so serious a problem that it merits interference with individual privacy or familial autonomy? As occupational specialization is a corollary of industrialization, should college education be more and more a process in which specialists prepare their students to be specialists, or should the trend be met by an increasing emphasis on general education, preparing students not in specialized subject matter but in the conduct and strategy of inquiry itself? How does a democratic society function in an era of mass production and distribution of information: Is the town meeting concept infinitely expandable? Might we poll citizens regularly and frequently on major policy decisions, or do voters hope simply to chart the main drift when they choose leaders and legislators and to review and evaluate over-all results at the next election?

In attempting to understand major social trends and to cope with the value dilemmas that are so often the by-products of social change, people run repeatedly into three large general questions: (1) What do social scientists know about the process of social change? (2) What is the nature of social man; how do his perceptions and beliefs affect his behavior in the face of change? (3) How free is man to influence his own destiny; does he simply respond to his social environment, or does he help to shape it? This brief final chapter offers a few comments on each.

The Components of Social Change

Modern social science is based to a great extent on ideas and information growing out of classical social theories of change. The nineteenth-century theorists are important contributors to our knowledge not because they were precise or even correct—their theories were often wrong and frequently untestable. Their value lies in the fact that they raise large questions and suggest directions for social-science research.

Marx predicted that, in industrial societies, the middle class would diminish and polarize; it has grown and not polarized. He predicted that the revolution would occur in highly industrialized societies; it has come to Russia and China but not to England, Japan, or the United States. Where it has come, it has neither eliminated internal conflicts nor created a classless society, as predicted. But Marx's theorizing has spawned generations of research on social stratification: studies of the ranking process, the nature of systems of rank and their consequences in occupations, education, income, and style of life in military, political, business, and educational organizations.

Spengler, Maine, Spencer, and many others have made similar contributions. Although their grandiose single-factor theories of change have usually been either untestable or discredited, their thinking has pointed the way toward empirical investigation of the process of change. Contemporary social scientists recognize that change can originate in any institutional area: demographic, educational, economic, political, or ideological. Furthermore, they are able to identify some of the more specific attributes of change situations with far more precision than were their theoretical forebears.

For example, social scientists know that the more heterogeneous the society, the more likely social change is to occur. This statement means that change occurs more frequently within an open class than within a caste, more frequently in voluntary associations than in clans, more frequently in urban environments than in rural ones. The more different points of view available and the more groups with conflicts of interest, the more likely is change.

A corollary is that the more any given change seems to pose a threat to traditional cultural values, the greater will be the resistance to it. People are particularly likely to resist changes that they see as forced upon their group or society by outsiders. As armies of occupation know (and as Americans have seen in the case of Office of Education guidelines for desegregation in the Deep South), changes that seem to be imposed from the outside are likely to be greeted with overt compliance and covert resistance.

When people want change, however, they can absorb massive alterations in the fabric of their society with minimal difficulty. Change requires adjustment and is to some extent necessarily hard on people. But people often do accept change with alacrity when it will demonstrably make life more secure (polio vaccine), less costly (nylon instead of silk hose), easier (electric refrigerator), or more fun (television).

Who spearheads change? Who are the people most likely to bring innovation to a society, resist its implications least, adapt to its consequences most readily, and become merchants of change? The young, of course, are receptive to change, in part because they have less investment in the traditional social structure. Intellectuals, too, oriented as they are toward the evaluation of competing ideas and an acceptance of the worth of new knowledge, are likely to be positively oriented to change. Indeed, not only intellectuals and youth, but any marginal or deviant groups, are apt to constitute a vanguard for change. The impetus to alter the social structure seldom comes from those in control of it.

In England far more leaders of the world's first industrial revolution came from among the religious nonconformists than from any other single group, even though the nonconformists formed only seven or eight per cent of the population of England. Many other leaders came from the lowland Scots, who had come under the political and social domination of the English.

In Japan disaffected social groups led the way in modernization. In about 1600 one group of clans, the Tokugawa, gained dominance over the entire country and subjected other clans, the "outer clans," to political and social subordination. Under the Tokugawa a national peace was imposed; the warrior class, the Samurai, lost their traditional social position and also steadily declined in wealth. The move toward modernization, which fermented under the surface, led to the overthrow of the Tokugawa in 1868 and thereafter proceeded rapidly, led by Samurai and individuals from the outer clans.

In Colombia the Spanish conquerors inhabited three high valleys which are the sites of the four main present cities of Colombia. In two of these valleys they developed landed estates and became landed gentry or cattlemen. In the third, Antioquia, because the land was less suitable and because other activities were more attractive, they did not. During the eighteenth and nineteenth centuries, as the historical literature of the time shows, the gentry of the other two valleys looked down on the Antioqueños because they too had not become gentry, and the Antioqueños resented this attitude. Today it is the Antioqueños who are spearheading economic and political modernization throughout Colombia.

In India successive waves of migration over several millennia have resulted in the existence of a number of social groups who even today are very conscious of their historical differences from each other. It is probably significant that much of the effective modern business activity to date in India has been initiated by several of the minority social groups—the Parsis, the Marwari, and others. . . .

It appears that a traditional society turned the more readily to modernization if there was any articulate group of men in it with reason to be unhappy about their position. Feeling aggrieved, already questioning the values and attitudes of the traditional society, they were psychologically prepared to accept new ways of life as a means of proving their worth and gaining self-satisfaction, status, and prestige. Put another way, the traditional society, despite its surface of coherence and stability, was often marked by inner conflicts; and one of the effects of intrusion from without was often to permit those conflicts to take forms that contributed significantly to modernization.[1]*

These deviant, marginal, or dissatisfied groups, which are most likely to initiate and maintain the thrust for change, allow us to see in the large a basic characteristic that differentiates man from other animals: Rather than simply adapting to his environment, man adapts his environment to himself.

The Nature of Social Man

Man is a long way removed from his animal origins. Animals adjust to the environment in which they find themselves; they survive on its terms or perish. Man adapts the environment to his own ends; he manipulates his world. Not only keen-eyed people prosper; so do those who wear glasses. Gorillas have impressive muscles, but men have pulleys and pile drivers. Men transform uncongenial environments with heating plants and air-conditioning systems, with sprinklers, snowplows, irrigation ditches, and chemical fertilizers.

But man does far more than transform his physical environment with applied physics and chemistry. He also

* Max F. Millikan and Donald L. M. Blackmer, eds., *The Emerging Nations: Their Growth and United States Policy.* Copyright © 1961, Massachusetts Institute of Technology. Reprinted by permission of the publisher, Little, Brown and Company (Inc.).

alters his personal environment by adjusting his perceptions to suit his desires. He changes the true physical
world when he is able to; when he cannot satisfy his wants
by engineering, he changes what he believes. The vocabulary of psychology is a set of descriptions of men adapting
reality to their circumstances: repression, projection, sub-
limation. Psychologists catalogue the ways in which people modify their perceptions of what the world is like.

When man can come to grips with his needs by actually
changing the environment, he does so. But when he cannot
achieve such "realistic" satisfaction, he tends to take the other
path: to modify what he sees to be the case, what he thinks he
wants, and what he thinks others want.*

From their inventory of social science research findings,
Berelson and Steiner conclude that

. . . no matter how successful man becomes in dealing with his
problems, he still finds it hard to live in the real world, un-
diluted: to see what one really is, to hear what others really
think of one, to face the conflicts and threats really present, or,
for that matter, the bare human feelings.†

Man, then, can shape his physical environment by engineering and alter his psychological environment by se-
lective perception, defense mechanisms, and personally
satisfying redefinition of situations. But he can do one
other thing to cope with reality, and that course of action
is the central theme of this book: He can engage in social
organization. In meeting the five prerequisites for social

---

* Bernard Berelson and Gary A. Steiner, *Human Behavior: An
Inventory of Scientific Findings* (New York: Harcourt, 1964),
p. 664.
† *Ibid.*

survival, he can choose among alternative ways of organizing his society.

To replace personnel, men can structure their social organization to provide for the recruitment of immigrants or for monogamous families, polyandrous families, or polygynous families. The familial structure can be patriarchal or matriarchal, matrilocal or patrilocal. Seemingly endless sets of choices confront men as they organize to fulfill the essential functions of human society. How shall they organize their economic endeavor? What kind of political structure is most desirable? What ought to be the relationship between polity and economy? How can young people most effectively be educated to participate in the social order?

But perhaps the most haunting question to a generation sophisticated in social science is this one: Does what men prefer make any difference? Do the seeming decision points offer real choices, or is each succeeding move predetermined by a complex and irredeemable history? Do men live in the sort of world envisioned by Spencer, in which the history of a society courses through stages analogous to those of an organism, with societal birth, infancy, maturity, decay, and death? Is the web of social interaction spun so fine that there is no room for anything to happen save those events already determined by occurrences that have preceded them? Or has man a hand in his fate?

Freedom and Challenge

One possibility for philosophers to speculate upon is the complete absence of order, a universe in which nothing is related to anything else and prediction is impossible. If all events were consequences of some statistically random impulse, the levels of predictability that scientists achieve would be inconceivable. Scientists assume the existence of an ordered universe. They use checks on the reliability of their observations because the logic of the scientific method is based upon the presence of patterns: patterns of molecular structure, of temperature responses to pressure, of genetic inheritance, of human migration in response to economic opportunity. But do the presence of such patterns imply a partially determined, limited universe of possibilities or a totally determined, unchangeable equation?

Some see man as an object over which the waves of history wash. Whether he floats or sinks depends on the currents and the tides, not on any decision or action of his. Social scientists usually view the social structure itself as the source of man's social behavior. Sammy runs, they say, because of the social environment in which he was reared and runs the way he does because of the social context into which his past has propelled him. According to this view, man is controlled by social, economic, and political conditions; when he faces what he regards as a choice, his response is actually not only conditioned but also determined by what has gone before.

But recently some social scientists have begun to view man, not as tempest-tossed, but as capable of swimming against the current, or at least of mounting a log swept along by the stream of history, partly controlling his destination, depending on his own determination and skill. It is an image of man as a human being able to rearrange the parts of the universe into a new pattern, a person capable of seizing the initiative and embarking on a new course.

Scholars have come to this position from asking about the exceptions to their generalizations. Most wealthy Americans vote Republican; how, then, account for wealthy Democrats? Many narcotics addicts are products of slum environments, discrimination, deprivation, and broken homes; what explains people from the same environment who do not choose narcotics as a way of life? And who are the prosperous, middle-class people who do?

One explanation lies in the existence, even within the limits of class and cultural environments, of alternative norms of behavior. Man is in part responsible for what he does with the opportunities confronting him, for it is true that

. . . most social pressures to conform are localized and that men in modern society are able to choose their social environment, and hence the social forces to which they accommodate themselves. While only saints and the insane can live without belonging to one or more social groups, and to be secure in it requires following to some degree the precepts of the group, the question of *which* group to belong to is much more open to individual choice. The options remain limited: few Negroes as yet can move into white groups (and vice versa). But a person who leads a "deviant" life—let us say, a homosexual— can move to a neighborhood where his behavior would be quite acceptable and can limit his intimate social contacts to those that share his sexual preference. Similarly, those who find small towns and suburbia too oppressive can move to the city, or to less socially oppressive suburbs. To be sure, there is usually a cost, but the option to pay it and be freed from any particular conformity, or to refrain from paying and submit to group norms, is a choice many members of modern society make—and often the cost is not inordinate.*

* Amitai Etzioni, "Crime and Free Will," *Book Week*, October 30, 1966, pp. 6, 16.

Urban, industrial social structure is an enormous generator of social problems in contemporary America—naturally, for urbanism and industrialism are central characteristics of American society. Urbanization and industrialization in the United States provide a setting for and contribute to a host of problems: miles of decaying slum tenements, legions of undereducated and unemployed citizens, undertrained and undermanned police forces facing well-financed and elaborately organized crime as well as anarchic street rioting, a shrinking urban tax base for coping with a growing welfare clientele.

But urbanism and industrialization are also rich resources. They make possible an unprecedented quantity and quality of transportation and communication facilities. The aggregation of people and institutions permits a more efficient educational system for the identification and exploitation of talent. The very size of the potential audience and market facilitates the expansion and diversification of intellectual and cultural opportunities.

Contemporary America lives with the tension between the problems and the challenges. Can we learn to understand and live with urbanization and industrialization? Will we be defeated by the costs or inspired by the opportunities?

Freedom is a product of awareness: awareness of choice, of the possibilities, of alternatives. Seizing freedom is a matter of courage, of willingness to face alternatives and, on occasion, to pay the price of being different.

REFERENCES

Documentation of the data presented in each chapter and further information on related topics are available from these sources. More detailed statistics on population, education, religious denominations, social class differences, urbanization, and political and economic trends can be found, with references to pertinent United States Census publications, in Kimball Young and Raymond W. Mack, *Sociology and Social Life*, (3rd ed., New York: American Book, 1965), Parts II and III.

CHAPTER 1. The Scientific Revolution and the
Nervousness of Man

Francis R. Allen, Hornell Hart, Delbert C. Miller, William F. Ogburn, and Meyer F. Nimkoff. *Technology and Social Change.* New York: Appleton, 1957.
An analysis of the impact of technology and applied science on social organization.

Lyman Bryson, ed. *An Outline of Man's Knowledge of the Modern World.* New York: McGraw-Hill, 1960.
A compilation of summaries of knowledge from various disciplines, including an excellent analysis by S. M. Lipset of trends in American society.

James B. Conant. *Modern Science and Modern Man.* New York: Columbia University Press, 1952 (reprinted, Garden City: Doubleday, 1955).
An excellent brief history of the development of science in this

century, with a thoughtful discussion of the relationship between science and human morals and conduct.

George A. Lundberg. *Can Science Save Us?* New York: Longmans, 1947.
A stimulating discussion of the prospects and difficulties of using social science to help present-day man solve some of his most pressing problems.

Margaret Mead, ed. *Cultural Patterns and Technical Change.* New York: New American Library, 1955.
A manual prepared for UNESCO by the World Federation for Mental Health. It deals with the impact of modern technology on nonindustrialized societies.

C. Wright Mills. *The Sociological Imagination.* New York: Oxford, 1959.
A contention that sociologists should work at the intersection of biography and history and a critique of major trends within the sociological "establishment."

Arnold M. Rose. *Theory and Method in the Social Sciences.* Minneapolis: University of Minnesota Press, 1954.
An excellent discussion of the status and prospects of sociology as a problem-solving discipline.

W. L. Thomas, Jr., ed. *Man's Role in Changing the Face of the Earth.* Chicago: University of Chicago Press, 1956.
A symposium covering topics from biological and physiographic to social and cultural change.

CHAPTER 2. Social Organization and Survival

Stuart Chase. *The Proper Study of Mankind.* Rev. ed. New York: Harper, 1956.
A stimulating account of the relatively recent advances in the social sciences.

Kingsley Davis. *Human Society.* New York: Macmillan, 1949.
An excellent general statement of the boundaries and contents of sociology.

George C. Homans. *The Human Group*. New York: Harcourt, 1950.

A fresh analysis of several basic studies of primary human groups, which provides a splendid introduction to what sociologists do and how they do it.

Francis L. K. Hsu. *Clan, Caste and Club: A Study of Chinese, Hindu and American Ways of Life*. Princeton: Van Nostrand, 1963.

An anthropologist's contrast of three cultures: one supernaturally oriented, one situation-centered, and one individualistic.

Clyde Kluckhohn. *Mirror for Man*. New York: McGraw-Hill, 1944 (reprinted, New York: Fawcett Premier Books, 1960).

The finest nontechnical introduction to modern anthropology.

Raymond W. Mack and George W. Baker. *The Occasion Instant: The Structure of Social Responses to Unanticipated Air Raid Warnings*. Washington, D.C.: National Academy of Sciences—National Research Council, 1961.

A research study concluding that the primary factor influencing the likelihood of group survival in a crisis is the way in which the group is organized.

Harold G. Wolff. "A Scientific Report on What Hope Does for Man." *Saturday Review*, 11 (1957), 44–5.

A summary of what is known about sense of purpose and survival.

CHAPTER 3. Births, Deaths, and Families: Traits and Trends

Donald J. Bogue. *The Population of the United States*. New York: Free Press, 1959.

A basic reference that presents, clearly and comprehensively, a description of the social characteristics of the population of the United States, with an analysis of the trends altering this composition.

Julia S. Brown. "A Comparative Study of Deviations from Sexual Mores." *American Sociological Review*, 17 (1952), 135–46.

A discussion of the varying severity of punishment for violations of sexual taboos in 110 nonliterate societies.

Paul C. Glick. *American Families.* New York: Wiley, 1957.
A very good description of the demographic and structural characteristics of the American family, based on data from the Census.

Philip M. Hauser and Otis Dudley Duncan, eds. *The Study of Population: An Inventory and Appraisal.* Chicago: University of Chicago Press, 1959.
A review of the status of demography as a science, also concerned with the interrelations of demography and other system variables in sociology.

William Petersen. *Population.* New York: Macmillan, 1961.
Includes, in addition to coverage of fertility, morbidity, mortality rates, and so forth, one chapter on the population of primitive peoples, another on population of preindustrial civilizations, and one on population during the Industrial Revolution.

Hyman Rodman, ed. *Marriage, Family, and Society.* New York: Random House, 1965.
A first-rate collection of readings, informed by the editor's developed commentary.

Ralph Thomlevian. *Population Dynamics.* New York: Random House, 1965.
An excellent, broad-ranging textbook on all principal aspects of demography, written from a sociological perspective.

Robert F. Winch. *The Modern Family.* 2nd ed. New York: Holt, 1963.
An outstanding treatment of contemporary American family structure.

CHAPTER 4. Education for What? American Traits and Trends

B. J. Chandler, Lindley J. Stiles, and John I. Kitsuse, eds. *Education in Urban Society.* New York: Dodd, Mead, 1963.
A collection of papers by social scientists dealing with the impact of urbanization on the organization of education.

James B. Conant. *The American High School Today: A First Report to Interested Citizens.* New York: McGraw-Hill, 1959.
A discussion of the characteristics of American education, the purposes of the comprehensive high school, size and location of schools as they influence comprehensiveness, and some specific recommendations.

Jacob W. Getzels and Philip W. Jackson. "Family Environment and Cognitive Style: A Study of the Sources of Highly Intelligent and Highly Creative Adolescents." *American Sociological Review,* 26 (1961), 351–59.
A report of research distinguishing between high I.Q. and creativity.

Neal Gross. *Who Runs Our Schools?* New York: Wiley, 1958.
A study of teachers' beliefs about educational administration and educational goals and of the conflict of values over organizational objectives.

Raymond A. Mulligan. "Socio-economic Background and College Enrollment." *American Sociological Review,* 16 (1951), 188–96.
A report of research, conducted at Indiana University, on the impact of the G.I. Bill.

Bernard Rosenberg and David Manning White, eds. *Mass Culture: The Popular Arts in America.* New York: Free Press, 1957.
Discussions of the impact of the mass media on the socialization process, with analyses of comic books, magazines, detective fiction, movies, television, and advertising as molders of cultural norms, attitudes, and social behavior.

Nevitt Sanford, ed. *The American College: A Psychological and Social Interpretation of the Higher Learning.* New York: Wiley, 1962.
A set of articles on student society and culture, student performance, and the effects of college education.

Robert R. Sears, Eleanor E. Maccoby, and Harry Levin. *Patterns of Child Rearing.* Evanston: Row, Peterson, 1957.
An analysis of data collected through interviews of 379 Ameri-

can mothers on how they reared their children from birth to kindergarten age.

John W. M. Whiting and Irvin L. Child. *Child Training and Personality: A Cross-Cultural Study.* New Haven: Yale University Press, 1953.

A comparison, among a wide range of nonliterate peoples, of socialization, fixation, the origins of fear and guilt, and related matters.

CHAPTER 5. The Production and Distribution of Abundance

Adolph A. Berle, Jr., and Gardiner C. Means. *The Modern Corporation and Private Property.* New York: Macmillan, 1933.

A classic study of the concentration of corporate wealth and the managerial revolution.

Robert Dubin. *The World of Work: Industrial Society and Human Relations.* Englewood Cliffs: Prentice-Hall, 1958.

A fine treatment of the organization of work in contemporary industrial society.

John Kenneth Galbraith. *The Affluent Society.* Boston: Houghton Mifflin, 1958.

Poses the question of whether an economic theory based on an economy of scarcity is relevant to the problems of a society of plenty.

Michael Harrington. *The Other America: Poverty in the United States.* Baltimore: Penguin, 1963.

An analysis of poverty in the United States as a self-perpetuating culture.

Edward S. Mason, ed. *The Corporation in Modern Society.* Cambridge, Mass.: Harvard University Press, 1959.

A stimulating collection of readings on the structure of the corporation and its impact on other organizations.

Edgar May. *The Wasted Americans.* New York: Harper, 1964.

An inquiry into why millions of Americans live on welfare in the midst of affluence.

Wilbert E. Moore. *The Conduct of the Corporation.* New York: Random House, 1963.
A fine analysis of the role and responsibilities of the corporation.

David Riesman. *Individualism Reconsidered.* New York: Free Press, 1954 (reprinted, Garden City: Doubleday, 1955).
A collection of essays, two of which, "Values in Context" and "New Standards for Old: From Conspicuous Consumption to Conspicuous Production," are pertinent to the material in this chapter.

W. W. Rostow. *The Stages of Economic Growth: A Non-Communist Manifesto.* Cambridge, Eng.: Cambridge University Press, 1960.
A description of the process of evolution to, and the characteristics of, a mass-consumption society.

W. S. Woytinsky and E. S. Woytinsky. *World Population and Production: Trends and Outlook.* New York: Twentieth Century Fund, 1953.
A broad survey of the collective resources and the economic performance and promise of the nations of the world.

CHAPTER 6. The Politics of Industrialization and the
Industrialization of Politics

Adolph A. Berle, Jr. *Power Without Property: A New Development in American Political Economy.* New York: Harcourt, 1959.
An analysis of the social consequences of the separation of ownership and proprietorship.

Kenneth E. Boulding. *Conflict and Defense: A General Theory.* New York: Harper, 1962.
Convinced that war is often a consequence of deficient social theory, Boulding draws upon various sources and disciplines to build a general theory of conflict.

William J. Lederer. *A Nation of Sheep.* New York: Norton, 1961 (reprinted, New York: Fawcett Crest Books, 1962).

> An expression of concern over the loss of individual freedom through government directive and secrecy.

Seymour Martin Lipset. *Political Man.* Garden City: Doubleday Anchor Books, 1963.

> A series of studies of the social bases of contemporary politics.

Raymond W. Mack. "Do We Really Believe in the Bill of Rights?" *Social Problems,* 3 (1956), 264–71.

> A research study of the extent to which university students accept the provisions of the first ten amendments to the Constitution when they are not aware of the source of the statements.

Hanan C. Selvin and Warren O. Hagstrom. "Determinants of Support for Civil Liberties." *British Journal of Sociology,* 11 (1960), 51–73.

> An exploration of the social characteristics of people with strong commitments to civil liberties.

Gresham M. Sykes. *The Society of Captives.* Princeton: Princeton University Press, 1958.

> A study of a maximum-security prison as an example of the interplay of social forces when the exercise of power nears its extreme in a system of total social control.

CHAPTER 7.   The American Dream and the American Dilemma

Hazel Gaudet Erskine. "The Polls: Race Relations." *Public Opinion Quarterly,* 26 (1962), 137–48.

> A valuable summary of what was learned by public-opinion polling of American attitudes on race relations between 1942 and 1962.

Gerhard Lenski. *The Religious Factor.* Garden City: Doubleday, 1961.

> An analysis of the interplay between religious affiliation and role behavior in other institutional areas as revealed in the Detroit Area Study.

James H. Leuba. "Religious Beliefs of American Scientists." *Harper's*, 169 (1934), 291–300.

A study of trends in the percentage of scientists who declared belief in God and immortality.

Raymond W. Mack. *Race, Class, and Power*. New York: American Book, 1963.

A collection of research articles exploring the tension among minority status, stratification, and American values.

Gunnar Myrdal, *et al. An American Dilemma: The Negro Problem and Modern Democracy*. New York: Harper, 1944.

A complete description and incisive analysis of the cultural paradox provided by the descendants of slaves in an equalitarian society.

Elizabeth K. Nottingham. *Religion and Society*. New York: Random House, 1954.

An excellent summary of the social-science literature on the nature and organization of religion and its consequences.

R. H. Tawney. *Religion and the Rise of Capitalism*. New York: Harcourt, 1936.

An analysis of the historical setting that proved congenial for the Industrial Revolution.

Melvin M. Tumin. *Desegregation: Resistance and Readiness*. Princeton: Princeton University Press, 1958.

Research on a fascinating problem: What are the social characteristics of people willing to resist violently the formally constituted authority of government when its rulings run contrary to strongly held personal values?

W. Lloyd Warner and James C. Abegglen. *Big Business Leaders in America*. New York: Harper, 1955.

A study comparing the social origins of more than 8,000 top executives in the largest firms in the United States with the top business leaders in 1928.

Max Weber. *The Protestant Ethic and the Spirit of Capitalism*. Trans. Talcott Parsons. New York: Scribner's, 1930.

The classic statement of the thesis that the Protestant Reformation and the rise of capitalism provided supportive environments for one another.

William H. Whyte, Jr. *The Organization Man.* New York: Simon & Schuster, 1956 (reprinted, Garden City: Doubleday, 1957).

A study of the shift in values that is accompanying the bureaucratization of American society; Chapter 2, "The Decline of the Protestant Ethic," is a particularly good analysis of changing social norms.

CHAPTER 8. The Conformity Question and the Search for Talent

Robert J. Alexander. *A Primer of Economic Development.* New York: Macmillan, 1962.

A discussion of the underdeveloped areas of the world and the techniques of economic development: the role of planning, the problems of the agricultural sector of the economy, the difficulty of raising capital, the place of foreign investment and foreign aid, and the peculiarities of entrepreneurship and of the labor force.

Howard S. Becker. *Outsiders: Studies in the Sociology of Deviance.* New York: Free Press, 1963.

A probing analysis of the norms governing two groups of people who reject the rules of the wider society: dance musicians and marijuana users.

Daniel Bell. *The End of Ideology.* New York: Free Press, 1960.

Contains a sociologically sophisticated look at social organization and deviance entitled "Crime as an American Way of Life."

William Dobriner. *Class in Suburbia.* Englewood Cliffs: Prentice-Hall, 1963.

Case studies suggesting that suburbs have varying life styles, depending on their class composition, and arguing that suburbs are an extension of urbanism, with its characteristics of cultural complexity and class awareness.

Robert E. L. Faris. "Reflections on the Ability Dimension in Human Society." *American Sociological Review,* 26 (1961), 835–43.

A challenging discussion of the prospects for an increase in collective mental ability in the United States.

REFERENCES

Scott A. Greer. *Governing the Metropolis*. New York: Wiley, 1962.
   A sociology of politics focusing on the problems arising from urbanism.

Oscar Lewis. *Five Families: Mexican Case Studies in the Culture of Poverty*. New York: Basic Books, 1959.
   A volume offering critical insights into the consequences of deprivation.

David C. McClelland. *The Achieving Society*. Princeton: Van Nostrand, 1961.
   An analysis of the need for achievement as the psychological factor motivating periods of rapid economic growth in both ancient and modern societies.

Robert K. Merton. *Social Theory and Social Structure*, rev. ed. New York: Free Press, 1957.
   A classic in the sociological literature dealing with group structure and its consequences.

C. Wright Mills. *White Collar*. New York: Oxford, 1951.
   A challenging study of the middle classes in America, especially thought-provoking in its argument that lower white-collar workers fail to use the political apparatus for their own interests because they choose to identify themselves with management.

Wilbert E. Moore and Arnold S. Feldman. *Labor Commitment and Social Change in Developing Areas*. New York: Social Science Research Council, 1961.
   The problems of social and cultural change wrought by the spread of industrialization, addressed by a number of social scientists.

William F. Ogburn. "Population, Private Ownership, Technology and the Standard of Living." *American Journal of Sociology*, 56 (1951), 314–9.
   An empirical study of the influence of social organization and technology on level of living.

David Riesman. *The Lonely Crowd: A Study of the Changing American Character*. New Haven: Yale University Press, 1950.
   A landmark in the theoretical discussion of conformity and its consequences.

191

John P. Roche and Milton M. Gordon. "Can Morality Be Legislated?" *The New York Times Magazine,* May 22, 1955, pp. 10, 42, 44, 49.
> A sound sociological analysis of a question that has arisen from ancient times to Prohibition and the Supreme Court's desegregation decision.

Muzafer Sherif, ed. *Intergroup Relations and Leadership.* New York: Wiley, 1962.
> Contains excellent summaries of theory and suggestions for research in the industrial, ethnic, cultural, and political arenas.

Edward G. Stockwell. "The Relationship between Population Growth and Economic Development." *American Sociological Review,* 27 (1962), 250–2.
> An empirical study of the extent to which rapid population increase impedes economic growth in underdeveloped nations.

Paul Studenski. *The Income of Nations.* New York: New York University Press, 1958.
> A valuable source of comparative data on national incomes and per capita income by country.

Robin M. Williams, Jr. *American Society: A Sociological Interpretation,* 2nd ed. New York: Knopf, 1960.
> A survey of major groups and institutions of American society.

Robert C. Woods. *Suburbia: Its People and Their Politics.* Boston: Houghton Mifflin, 1963.
> An insightful analysis of the political and social behavior of suburbanites.

CHAPTER 9. Social Change and Free Men

Howard S. Becker, ed. *Social Problems.* New York; Wiley, 1966.
> A collection of essays by several scholars on major social issues from urbanization to world peace.

Kai T. Erikson. *Wayward Puritans: A Study in the Sociology of Deviance.* New York: Wiley, 1966.
> A historical-sociological study of seventeenth-century New Eng-

land, pointing out the value of deviant behavior for human society.

Amitai Etzioni and Eva Etzioni, eds. *Social Change: Sources, Patterns, and Consequences.* New York: Basic Books, 1964.
A reader containing fifty selections, historical and contemporary, on social change.

David Matza. *Delinquency and Drift.* New York: Wiley, 1964.
An analysis of the nature and extent of conformity among delinquents and of how they choose or drift among alternative modes of behavior.

Wilbert E. Moore. *Social Change.* Englewood Cliffs: Prentice-Hall, 1963.
A discussion of change as a regularity, or normal part of social systems.

NAME INDEX

Abegglen, James C., 141, 189
Adler, Mortimer J., 65
Alexander, Robert J., 190
Allen, Francis R., 181
Allen, Frederick Lewis, 98–9

Baker, George W., 183
Becker, Howard S., xii, 190,
  192
Bell, Daniel, 190
Berelson, Bernard, 176
Berle, Adolph A., Jr., 186–7
Blackmer, Donald L. M., 174–
  175
Bogue, Donald J., 183
Boulding, Kenneth E., 187
Brown, Julia S., 42, 183
Bryson, Lyman, 181

Calvin, John, 133
Chandler, B. J., 184
Chase, Stuart, xv, 182
Child, Irvin L., 186
Comte, Auguste, vii
Conant, James B., 181, 185

Darwin, Charles, vii, 7
Davis, Kingsley, xii, 9, 38,
  182
Dewey, John, 65

Dobriner, William, 190
Dubin, Robert, xii, 186
Duncan, Otis Dudley, 184
Durkheim, Emile, 26

Erikson, Kai T., 192
Erskine, Hazel Gaudet, 188
Etzioni, Amitai, 179, 193
Etzioni, Eva, 193

Faris, Robert E. L., 167, 190
Feldman, Arnold S., xii, 191
Fischer, John, 66, 69
Flood, Daniel J., 129

Galbraith, John Kenneth, 186
Getzels, Jacob W., 67, 185
Glick, Paul C., 184
Gordon, Milton M., 192
Greer, Scott A., xii, 191
Gross, Neal, 185

Hagstrom, Warren O., 188
Harrington, Michael, 186
Hart, Hornell, 181
Hauser, Philip M., 38, 40, 157,
  158, 184
Herring, Harriet L., xii
Homans, George C., xii, 183

SUBJECT INDEX

A NOTE ON THE TYPE

The text of this book is set in Caledonia, a typeface designed by W(illiam) A(ddison) Dwiggins for the Mergenthaler Linotype Company in 1939. Dwiggins chose to call his new typeface Caledonia, the Roman name for Scotland, because it was inspired by the Scotch types cast about 1833 by Alexander Wilson & Son, Glasgow type founders. However, there is a calligraphic quality about this face that is totally lacking in the Wilson types. Dwiggins referred to an even earlier typeface for this "liveliness of action"—one cut around 1790 by William Martin for the printer William Bulmer. Caledonia has more weight than the Martin letters, and the bottom finishing strokes (serifs) of the letters are cut straight across, without brackets, to make sharp angles with the upright stems, thus giving a "modern face" appearance.

W. A. Dwiggins (1880-1956) was born in Martinsville, Ohio, and studied art in Chicago. In 1904 he moved to Hingham, Massachusetts, where he built a solid reputation as a designer of advertisements and as a calligrapher. He began an association with the Mergenthaler Linotype Company in 1929, and over the next twenty-seven years designed a number of book types for that firm. Of especial interest are the Metro series, Electra, Caledonia, Eldorado, and Falcon. In 1930, Dwiggins first became interested in marionettes, and through the years made many important contributions to the art of puppetry and the design of marionettes.

Typography by Vincent Torre.